MAINTAINING A SENSE OF PLACE

A Citizen's Guide to Community Preservation

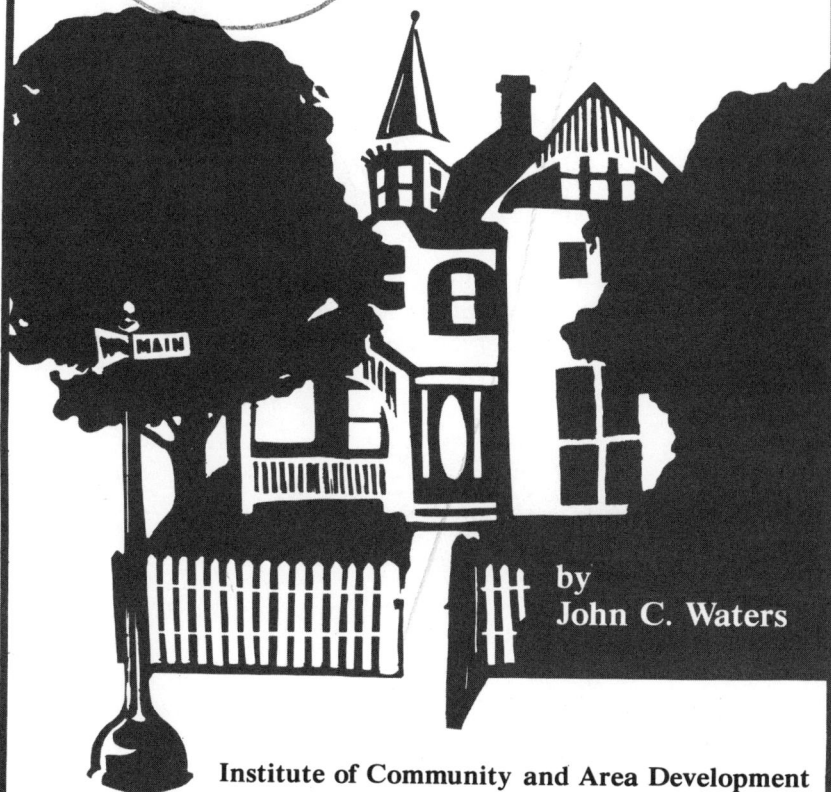

by
John C. Waters

Institute of Community and Area Development

PuBPoL
Water, J
mSop
1983

Maintaining a Sense of Place
a citizen's guide to community preservation

editors: Ruth Carpenter, Rebecca McCarthy
proofreading: Nancy Condon
production: Janet Walker
cover and design: Reid McCallister

Library of Congress Cataloging in Publication Data

Waters, John C.
  Maintaining a sense of place.
      3 Community life — Georgia
  1. Historic sites—Law and legislation—Georgia.
  2. Historic sites—Georgia—Conservation and restoration.
  I. The University of Georgia. Institute of Community and Area Development. II. Title.
  KFG398.9.W37 1983   344.758'094   83-12810
  ISBN 0-911847-00-6   347.580494

Foreword

Since World War II, the interest of individuals and communities in saving old buildings and their settings has increased from year to year, on the national, state, and community level.

Congress created the National Trust for Historic Preservation in 1949 and enacted the National Historic Preservation Act of 1966. Both 1976 and 1981 saw the creation of federal tax incentives for individuals rehabilitating historic structures.

On the state level, the Georgia General Assembly enacted the 1980 Georgia Historic Preservation Act, which authorized the creation of historic preservation commissions.

Communities concerned with protecting the past to enrich the future have turned to design review as the standard mechanism for implementing municipal preservation policy. Historic zoning, architectural review boards, and preservation commissions have been used to implement design review in communities across the country.

The Institute of Community and Area Development (ICAD) has been involved in the preservation process since 1969, when it helped sponsor a citizens' conference on historic resource protection. ICAD later provided technical assistance to Georgia legislators drafting the act.

Currently, ICAD advises and counsels historic preservation organizations—on many different levels—across the state. This book continues those efforts by seeking to acquaint readers with the details of the Georgia Historic Preservation Act as well as with ways in which they can take advantage of the provisions of the act within their own communities.

Ernest E. Melvin
Director
Institute of Community
and Area Development

Contents

Appendices

Preface

Within the past half century, Americans have come to appreciate the contributions historic resources have made to their daily lives. They have recognized the spectrum of benefits that preservation provides to both individuals and society at large. These benefits are economic, social, and aesthetic. A more specific classification would enumerate the following:

1. Preservation, enhancement, and maintenance of existing urban amenities, too costly to replace once destroyed;
2. the recycling, or adaptive re-use, of old buildings and neighborhoods for continued use and benefit;
3. the maintenance, or enhancement, of property values;
4. the retention of the indigenous character and sense of time and place which provides identity to the community and its residents;
5. enhancement of the aesthetic quality of the community and promotion of support for urban design standards; and
6. guidance of the orderly growth and development of the community.

The ultimate impact of these benefits is the enhancement of the quality of environments as well as the quality of life for an area's inhabitants.

Local government protection of historic resources developed from a strong belief in the ability and responsibility of local governments to provide for the welfare and well-being of citizens. Local governmental protection is a means of providing the various benefits mentioned previously.

The evolution of this preservation concept has been gradual and its application has been slow. Almost 50 years separate the creation of the nation's first preservation ordinance and the 1980 Georgia Historic Preservation Act.

However, few Georgians are aware of the 1980 legislation, its provisions, or its procedures. They do not use the act to their community's advantage. Helping to correct this situation is the intent of this book.

John C. Waters
Athens, Georgia
December 1983

I
Evolution of the Preservation Concept

Every community has buildings that represent its past. Buildings 50 years old, or older, link past and present generations and represent the history of the community. These buildings are often described as having historic significance, which may be local, statewide, or national. The extent to which a building is recognized as historic—and is thereby worthy of preservation—often determines whether it survives as a part of the community.

Roots of Preservation in the 19th Century

In the past, functional and economic value determined whether a building was maintained, allowed to deteriorate, or demolished. However, during the 19th century, historic significance emerged as a new factor in building evaluation. Buildings recognized as historically significant were those associated with important events or individuals in history.

Before 1876, most of the events and individuals considered significant related to the Revolutionary War and the founding of the nation. As time passed and the memory of this period dimmed, many people began to feel that identifying historic sites and structures related to the founding of the nation could be a way to educate citizens, children, and immigrants and to inspire them with patriotism. Many older buildings identified with particular events in history assumed a new functional value beyond that of the normal work-a-day world; they became symbols of the past and inspirations for the future.

As citizens began to understand and value the significance of historic buildings, support for preservation grew across America. Led by historic and patriotic groups, a number of historic structures were preserved, often as public museums. Local groups frequently marked the sites of demolished significant buildings with commemorative tablets.

Preservation in the 20th Century

Preservation, based upon historic association, continued into the twentieth century. However, the preservation concept radically changed, especially from 1910 to 1931. New England resident William Sumner Appleton recognized that many historic buildings were architecturally significant, regardless of what had occurred within their walls. Thus, Appleton introduced the concept of architectural significance, unrelated to specific historic events, as a basis for preservation. He founded the Society for the Preservation of New England Antiquities (SPNEA).

Subsequently, older structures were viewed as aesthetic and utilitarian expressions of certain historic periods, ones that the contemporary community should retain as symbols of its past. Appleton's interest in preserving buildings led to his introducing another idea. He recognized that all historic buildings could not be preserved as museums only for exhibition purposes. To solve this problem, Appleton introduced the idea of keeping historic structures in current use with adequate safeguards against damaging changes. This proposal involved acquiring control of significant buildings through gift, purchase, or other means; restoring the properties; and then renting them to tenants under restrictions designed to safeguard the architectural integrity of the structures.

The value of this approach was the opportunity of using historic structures as a part of continuing community life, instead of isolating them as objects of inspiration and veneration. Appleton's views found many supporters and his organization became an important force in the restoration and preservation of numerous properties in the New England area.

The Williamsburg Example

A year after a 1926 visit to Williamsburg, Virginia, John D. Rockefeller, Jr., decided to restore and preserve the most significant portions of the historic colonial capitol. The resultant development of what is now Colonial Williamsburg involved both restorations of existing colonial buildings and carefully researched reconstructions of major buildings that had not survived. This extraordinary undertaking introduced the concept of preservation on a communitywide basis, endorsing the idea of evaluating buildings in relation to surrounding structures.

In restoring Williamsburg, Rockefeller introduced America to the outdoor museum, an idea that had originated in Sweden in 1891. The restored town became a setting for the interpretation of colonial life and history. Removed from the realm of continued community use, Williamsburg was operated as a museum preserved for exhibition. Williamsburg has given Americans an unparalleled opportunity to discover and appreciate their 18th-century aesthetic and political heritage.

Communitywide preservation was beginning to interest more Americans. In this respect, Williamsburg fostered a new appraisal of preservation possibilities within communities. Of course, 20th-century development often prevented citywide preservation because the museum concept was inconsistent with the continued functioning of viable communities. However, recognition of the available opportunities for the preservation of areas within communities set the stage for municipal governments to adopt preservation policies.

The Charleston Example

When the 1931 South Carolina legislature approved the "Old and Historic District of Charleston," it created the first historic district in the United States. It also designated area preservation by architectural control as a legitimate concern of state and municipal government.

Drawing from the example of Williamsburg, this legislation recognized that the value of preserving the historic and aesthetic character of entire areas was far greater than that derived from individual structures and sites. Such areas were described as those in which a large proportion of the buildings had been constructed during a significant architectural period, or had important associations with the history of the community, state, or nation.

The creation of this first historic district was based upon principles of municipal zoning. Consistent with the purposes of preservation, this type of zoning included architectural control. As a preservation device, architectural control made it possible to prevent the construction of new buildings that were incompatible with old buildings, or the alteration of existing ones, which could detract from the aesthetic quality of a designated historic district. Architectural control also made it possible to protect the harmonious exterior relationships of buildings, without affecting how the interiors of buildings were actually used.

Following the Charleston example, New Orleans created the Vieux Carre Commission in 1936 to preserve the French Quarter as an historic district. Little activity concerning the establishment of municipal historic districts occurred until the post-World War II boom in construction and development, along with an increased volume of automobile traffic, threatened the older portions of many cities. This increasing pressure precipitated the creation of historic districts in Alexandria, Virginia; Winston-Salem, North Carolina; Georgetown in the District of Columbia; Natchez, Mississippi; and Annapolis, Maryland.

In 1965, fewer than 100 communities had enacted ordinances creating historic districts. Today, however, more than 50 years after the passage of the first ordinance, more than 800 communities have some type of preservation policy.

Landmark v. Historic District Ordinances

Landmark and historic district ordinances are two approaches to the development of municipal preservation policy that reflect public interest in historic preservation. Both types of ordinance concern the preservation of structures through the use of architectural control, and both are administered by appointed commissions. However, the two approaches differ in both scope and authority.

An historic district ordinance controls a specific area, or district, in which a majority of structures are of architectural or historic significance. Generally, historic district commissions control the appearance of all buildings within an historic district, regardless of the architectural or historic significance of each building. This control includes the authority to approve or disapprove both the demolition or exterior alteration of significant buildings and the design of proposed new buildings. The commission may sometimes even have the ability to permanently bar disapproved demolition or alteration.

By comparison, a landmark ordinance covers an entire city or county, depending on the legislative jurisdiction of the enacting government. The buildings protected by a landmark ordinance are usually individual structures randomly located within a city or county, although some landmark ordinances do provide for district designations. As a general rule, the landmark ordinance does not provide control of areas adjacent to significant structures, especially in regard to review of proposed new construction. Usually the landmark ordinance is limited to imposing a stay of demolition or alteration of significant structures as opposed to the permanent banning of such action by the historic district ordinance.

In summary, the landmark approach considers significant structures as isolated objects within the community. The historic district approach is concerned with maintaining environmental compatibility within neighborhoods or areas. The historic district ordinance often provides a greater degree of protection for significant buildings as well as the added opportunity to insure that new development is aesthetically compatible with the old.

As we have indicated, historic preservation began in the 19th century, when private citizens worked to preserve individual structures related to the birth of the nation. Over the years, practices and principles of historic preservation have evolved dramatically. The 19th-century concern for the protection of historic structures has grown into a 20th-century concept that embraces architectural significance, applies to entire communities, and has become an element of municipal policy.

Thus, preservation has evolved from concept to policy, from a concern of individuals to a concern of municipal government. This evolution has produced a growing awareness of both the benefits of preservation and the responsibility of government to secure those benefits for the common good of all citizens.

II
Evolution of Historic Preservation in Georgia

As part of the South, Georgia has always been an area whose citizens were imbued with a strong sense of place and history as well as an understanding of the relationship of the two. It seems Georgia has also always been a society of inner-directed individuals who eschewed group action as long as individual efforts could achieve desired results.

State and National Trends and Influences

Within this context, one can appreciate the celebration of the centennial of James Oglethorpe's 1733 landing as the citizens' first collective expression of the importance of their state's past. Perhaps a new appreciation of the value of collective endeavors, stemming from the 1833 centennial celebration, led to the founding of the Georgia Historical Society in Savannah in 1839.

Growth of Historical Societies

Established "to collect, preserve, and diffuse information about the history of the State of Georgia in all its various departments, and American history generally, and to create an historical library for the use of its members and others,"[1] the Georgia Historical Society received public endorsement. Such support enabled the Society by 1849 to construct and occupy for its headquarters and library a building designed by John Norris.

While the Georgia Historical Society continued to grow and prosper, other historical organizations in the nation often placed monuments or markers to commemorate sites or important persons. Many of these efforts were concerned with the birth of the nation. Thus, in 1850, it was not surprising that the State of New York purchased Hasbrouck House, site of Washington's last headquarters during the Revolution, to preserve it as a symbol of our nation's past. Similarly, in 1853, when the home of George Washington appeared to be in danger, South Carolinian Ann Pamela Cunningham organized the Mount Vernon Ladies' Association and, on their behalf, directed a nationwide campaign to raise money to purchase the property.

A number of Georgians probably contributed to the purchase price of Mount Vernon because Philoclea C. Eve, of Georgia, was one of the first individuals to join Cunningham in her campaign to solicit funds from the 29 existing states and the District of Columbia. Eve was the designated vice regent for Georgia.[2] The campaign culminated in 1858, when Cunningham led citizens to rescue the endangered homeplace of the nation's first president.[3]

Immediately following the War Between the States,[4] preservation in Georgia was all too often related to rebuilding society. However, soon individuals, organizations, and entire communities across the state were involved in efforts to commemorate those who served the Confederacy, efforts that continued throughout the last quarter of the 19th century. Today, in mute testimony to this concern, hardly a courthouse square or city park in Georgia is without its Confederate monument.

In Savannah in 1871, the growth of the library of the Georgia Historical Society forced the organization from its headquarters until a larger structure could be constructed. Completed in 1875, the society's new building was named Hodgson Hall.

Effects of the 1876 Centennial

Though Georgians were largely concerned with other matters at this time, in 1876 in Philadelphia the nation celebrated the centennial of its founding. At the center of this celebration was the Centennial Exposition, which featured numerous displays and exhibits. One of these exhibits, "An Old-Time New England Farmhouse," duplicated the interior of a 1776 log cabin and served to stimulate national interest in both preserving buildings and using them as interpretive museums complete with authentic furnishings.

Perhaps the greatest impact of the Centennial Exposition, however, was the enthusiasm it generated for the nation's past, particularly the Revolution, and the sense of patriotism it cultivated.

Numerous groups formed, many of them seeking to preserve structures that would imbue visitors with patriotism. Interest continued
to grow; by 1890, the nation was experiencing a surge of patriotism.
One manifestation of this mounting patriotism was the 1890 founding of the Daughters of the American Revolution (DAR).

Because it was one of the original 13 colonies, Georgia had some
of the first DAR chapters. The policy of the DAR—then and
now—was to encourage the preservation of sites connected with
the American Revolution. It was, therefore, only a matter of time
before a chapter put these principles into practice. Seven years
after the 1890 creation of the DAR, the Augusta chapter proposed
purchasing Meadow Garden, home of George Walton, a signer of
the Declaration of Independence. In dedicating this site in 1901, the
DAR brought Georgia back into the mainstream of the preservation
movement of that time.[5]

Governmental Interest in Preservation

The Georgia Department of Archives and History

In response to the growing interest in history, in 1918 the Georgia
General Assembly created the Department of Archives and History to collect and preserve artifacts. In addition to its curatorial
responsibilities, this department was also charged with stimulating
and encouraging the study of history and with keeping biographical
records on all Georgia public officials. Thus, 79 years after the
founding of the Georgia Historical Society by private citizens, the
concept of preserving historic records had become an institutional-
ized part of public policy.

U.S. Congress

Congressional interest in historic preservation officially began in
1889, when Congress authorized the establishment of the Casa
Grande Reservation in Arizona to save prehistoric adobe ruins.

Shortly thereafter, Congress authorized the purchase of several
battlefields for development as interpretive facilities and as memo-
rials to war casualties. Georgia's Chickamauga Battlefield was first
selected in 1895. Congressional interest expanded to include protecting properties on federal lands, initiating a national survey of
significant properties, and realizing the need to involve the general
public in the protection of the national heritage.

When Congress passed the Historic Sites Act of 1935, its concern
was expanded to properties not publicly owned. The act authorized
a national survey of historic buildings. However, in time there was

widespread recognition of the need to involve the general public in protecting the nation's heritage.

The National Trust for Historic Preservation

To this end, Congress chartered in 1949 the National Trust for Historic Preservation as a national, nonprofit, private organization to encourage public participation in preserving sites, buildings, and objects significant in American history and culture. While given some federal funding, the National Trust was established as a membership organization dependent mostly upon dues-paying members and other donors for the support of its services.

These services included counseling and education on all aspects of preservation as well as property interpretation. Governed by a board of trustees who, in turn, were counseled by a board of advisors representing each state and territory, the National Trust very quickly became a clearinghouse for "grassroots" preservation problems and concerns.

Only a very few preservation-oriented organizations existed in Georgia before 1949, compared to the 131 now extant. This fact suggests that the National Trust has been a positive influence. With the creation of the National Trust, preservation achieved a higher level of legitimacy: that of a national goal, sanctioned by Congress, transcending the borders of individual states or the mores of any one particular society. Thus, establishing the Trust helped create a new climate of national support for individual and state agency preservation efforts.

The Georgia Historical Commission

Within this new preservation climate, the Georgia Historical Commission was established in 1951, a generation after the creation of the Department of Archives and History. Three major elements contributed to the creation of the Georgia Historical Commission: (1) the desire to erect a memorial to Crawford W. Long, the discoverer of ether; (2) the desire to promote tourism in Georgia; and (3) the desire to establish an historic marker program commemorating the War Between the States in Georgia.

Established by the General Assembly, the Commission had functions that included promoting a knowledge of the state from prehistory to the present; permanently preserving and marking sites; publicizing Georgia's history; coordinating the Commission's efforts with both state and federal agencies; and advising local entities on historic matters.

Described as "the pivotal force for historical preservation in the

State of Georgia from 1951 to 1973,"[6] the Georgia Historical Commission placed approximately 1,800 historic markers, as well as acquired, protected, and interpreted 20 sites.

Communities witnessed the organization of historic societies and foundations committed to protecting resources. However, perhaps as an expression of the traditional sense of individualism, various organizations, including the Georgia Historical Commission, tended to operate independently. There were no state monies for community projects—the money for local projects or programs was raised by local initiatives. State monies were spent only on projects of significance to the entire state.

This pattern was altered by the passage of the National Historic Preservation Act of 1966, the culmination of more than 75 years of federal interest in preservation.

The National Historic Preservation Act

With this act, Congress authorized a federal-state partnership for the protection of the nation's resources. The partnership was a part of Congress's declaration of preservation as an element of national policy, one worthy of financial support.

The act provided for: an expanded National Register of Historic Places; the allocation of cost-sharing funds to states for the preparation of comprehensive state surveys; the development of an environmental review process; the preparation and evaluation of nominations to the National Register; and the development of a grants-in-aid program for preservation projects.

The act also required the designation, by the states, of state liaison officers charged with responsibility for program administration. The designation of the director of the Georgia Historical Commission as state liaison officer made the Commission the focus of preservation planning activities within the state. The Commission was the agency through which the National Historic Preservation Act of 1966 was implemented within Georgia.

The act specifically mandated a federal-state partnership and provided matching grants for surveying and planning work. It rapidly became obvious that without a parallel partnership between the state agency and private organizations at the county or community level, reaping the full benefits of the legislation would be difficult.

Citizen Involvement
The Georgia Trust

Thus, what became the first of several succeeding annual

statewide preservation conferences was held in Athens in 1969,[7] in an effort to foster cooperation between all preservation-oriented entities within the state. Out of these annual statewide conferences grew the Georgia Trust for Historic Preservation. Incorporated in 1973, the Trust is a statewide citizen's organization that continues the annual statewide preservation conference as the focus of its annual membership meeting.

The Georgia Conservancy

One of the sponsors of the initial 1969 Athens preservation meeting was the Georgia Conservancy, organized only two years earlier to protect Georgia's environment. The Conservancy recognized the importance of preservation and established an Historic Sites Committee. However, the Conservancy made its greatest contributions to preservation endeavors by promoting the idea of a heritage trust.

The Georgia Heritage Trust

Initially established in 1972 by executive order, the Georgia Heritage Trust was sanctioned by a 1975 legislative act recognizing an urgent need to preserve important and endangered elements of Georgia's heritage, including historic, recreational, and natural resources, by direct purchase or through the acquisition of lesser property interests. The Trust was effectively funded from 1972 to 1979 with state appropriations of approximately $25 million, matched in some instances by federal funds and private donations. These monies have been used to buy more than 80,000 acres of significant property and to make grant awards to local governments.

Growth of Preservation Organizations

From both a national and statewide perspective, 1967 to 1976 can be described as a period of intense preservation concern and activity. Initiated by the passage of the National Historical Preservation Act of 1966 and concluded with the observance of the nation's bicentennial, this period was dominated by concern for history as well as for the quality of both the natural and manmade environments.

During this time, Congress recognized the relationship of these two concerns and enacted the National Environmental Policy Act in 1969. This act charged all federal agencies with responsibility to "preserve important, cultural, and natural aspects of our national heritage. . ." and required that they prepare detailed environmental impact statements for actions significantly affecting the quality of the human environment.

In response to the articulation of national policy by Congress, Georgians developed numerous citizens' organizations. The General Assembly, ever mindful of constituent concerns, enacted new statutes supporting preservation policy.

A recently published directory of historic and preservation organizations in Georgia identifies 131 local organizations within 96 counties.[8] The dates of origin are known for only 81 of these groups, but this information sufficiently documents the growing concern of citizens for their heritage.

As the accompanying chart shows, these 81 organizations have been created within a 35-year period following World War II. The growth rate of each succeeding decade has been at least twice that of the preceding period. Perhaps of even greater interest is the creation of 47 percent of the groups from 1967 to 1976. Additional growth after that period amounts to 37 percent of the total to date. Organizations created since the passage of the National Historic Preservation Act of 1966 total 84 percent of those created since the end of World War II.

Growth of historic and preservation organizations in Georgia 1946-1981[9]

period organized	number of groups	rate of growth– one every ...	percentage of whole
1945-1956	4	... 2 yr. 9 mo.	4.94 or 5%
1957-1966	9	... 13 months	11.11 or 11%
1967-1976	38	... 16 weeks	46.91 or 47%
1977-1981	30	... 7 weeks	37.04 or 37%
	81		100.00 or 100%

Response of the Georgia General Assembly

Legislation

The dramatic growth of interest during the 1967-1976 decade supported the creation of both the Georgia Conservancy and the Georgia Trust for Historic Preservation. In keeping with this expression of citizen concern, the General Assembly enacted the following:

(1) Georgia Antiquities Act of 1969, asserting state ownership and control of prehistoric and historic sites, ruins, and artifacts on public land, in navigable waters, and within three miles of the Georgia coast. The act also established the Office of State Archaeologist.

(2) Georgia Heritage Trust Act of 1975, creating legislative authorization for the Heritage Trust Program. The program had been created by executive order.

(3) Facade and Conservation Easements Act of 1976, providing individual property owners the opportunity to grant preservation easements to governmental and/or qualifying nonprofit organizations and stating that this encumbrance shall be reflected in the property tax assessment equal to the reduction in the property value represented by the value of the easement.

The bicentennial year was important in the General Assembly for those concerned with historic preservation. In addition to the Facade and Conservation Easements Act, two other preservation-related bills were considered: the Georgia Historic Preservation Enabling Act and a bill revising the State Constitution. To understand the relationship of these two pieces of legislation, one must look at what preservationists call "the Savannah experience."

The Savannah Experience

When James Oglethorpe landed at Savannah in 1733 to found the Colony of Georgia, he laid out a city that would later be recognized as the first planned city in America. For more than two centuries, this plan has survived. Today, Savannah is recognized as one of the preservation success stories of the nation.

However, the present conditions contrast with those of the first half of the century. During that dark period, the city's wealth of architecture was ignored; demolition and decay were the rule. Despite individual restoration efforts, widespread interest in preservation did not develop in Savannah until both the Wetter House and the City Market were demolished in the early 1950s. These demolitions, combined with the threatened demolition of the Davenport House, gave rise to the organization of the Historic Savannah Foundation, a nonprofit citizen's organization dedicated to the preservation and protection of the city's priceless historic resources—including houses, parks, and squares.

The Davenport House was saved. Encouraged by its success, the Historic Savannah Foundation moved to save other endangered properties. Soon the need for an architectural assessment survey

became evident, and the Foundation undertook a survey that ultimately evaluated 1,100 of Savannah's historic structures. Other
Foundation initiatives included creating a revolving fund for the
purchase of endangered buildings and promoting a local preservation ordinance.

Promoting the ordinance was not an easy undertaking. In the
absence of enabling legislation, it was necessary for local legislators to introduce a resolution to the General Assembly seeking
permission to hold a local referendum on historic zoning. The
resolution was considered courtesy legislation and was passed
easily because Savannah area legislators sponsored it.

When considered in conjunction with the 1968 general elections,
the referendum measure was overwhelmingly favored by Savan-
nahians and was passed by a large majority of the General Assembly. Nevertheless, one individual did not favor historic zoning—the
new mayor chosen in the same election.

So began a very difficult period of confrontation, persuasion, and
compromise involving the concept and application of historic zoning in Savannah. This period lasted almost five years. Finally, in
1973, the city adopted an historic zoning ordinance, requiring a
design review of changes to existing buildings and proposals for
new construction, as well as a stay of demolition on historic buildings.

State Legislation— Zoning

Prior to Savannah's referendum in 1968, the General Assembly
had enacted general planning enabling legislation that authorized
the creation of local zoning ordinances by cities and counties.
Although the legislation did not cite historic preservation as a basis
for zoning, it did include conservation as an allowable purpose for
zoning.

In reading the legislation, a number of local governments, most
notably Columbus, interpreted conservation as including historic
buildings and proceeded to enact local ordinances for the protection of historic structures and areas.

By the mid-1970s, however, there was considerable debate about
this interpretation, as well as about legislative intent. This debate
raised the specter of the potential unconstitutionality of local zoning for preservation purposes. The result was an undesirable situation in which opponents of preservation zoning could use the issue
of constitutionality to intimidate both local governments and citizens interested in the adoption of an historic zoning ordinance.

Because of its own interest in developing a local preservation ordinance, the Athens-Clarke Heritage Foundation contacted The University of Georgia's Institute of Community and Area Development (ICAD) in the mid-1970s. The foundation asked ICAD for help in developing state enabling legislation that would specifically empower local governments to zone for historic purposes, thus eliminating any question of constitutionality.

The result was the Georgia Historic Preservation Enabling Act. In addition to authorizing historic zoning by local governments, the act established minimum standards for the creation and operation of local preservation commissions.

Creation of the Georgia Historic Preservation Enabling Act

Representative Dorothy Felton (Republican, District 22, Atlanta) assisted the Athens-Clarke Heritage Foundation by introducing the enabling act proposal to the 1976 session of the General Assembly, where it became House Bill 327. The bill passed the House 152 to 3 but died in a senate committee.

However, a bill revising the State Constitution was passed during the same legislative session. This bill eliminated the need for specific legislation authorization for preservation zoning through the allocation of all zoning authority to local governments, except where the resources involved were vital to the state at large. In addition, the legislature retained the authority to set standards for zoning by the various governmental units.

It became obvious that, while the original purpose of the bill was no longer relevant, there was a need for minimum standards of historic resource protection. In addition, it was recognized that many local governments in Georgia did not have any form of zoning within their jurisdictions.

Subsequently, a decision was made to revise the original legislation to: (1) recognize that the original purpose of the bill—authorization of local preservation zoning authority—was no longer necessary, and (2) provide an alternative to zoning as a means of historic resource protection. Since there was a continuing need for minimum standards for the creation and operation of local preservation commissions, this portion of the original bill was retained.

Thus, plans were made for another campaign within the General Assembly. A part of those plans was the endorsement of the new legislative proposal by the Georgia Trust for Historic Preservation. In fact, the Trust's interest in the new proposal went beyond endorsement to sponsorship, as evidenced by its decision to initiate a lobbying effort at the state capitol. This interest was reinforced by the development of a preservation legislation network across the state. Representative Felton introduced the revised proposal to the 1978 session of the General Assembly. This proposal, named the Georgia Historic Preservation Act, was designated House Bill 457. The bill was ultimately passed in 1980 with several modifications. The most significant one exempted the Georgia Department of Transportation, its contractors, and local governments from the provisions of the act. Political necessities dictated the exemption—without it, the bill would not have passed.

The Georgia Historic Preservation Act

On April 8, 1980, Governor George Busbee signed into law the Georgia Historic Preservation Act of 1980. The bill had evolved from a need to establish the constitutionality of local preservation zoning to a need to develop an alternative to zoning, thus providing local governments with a choice about how they might protect historic resources within their jurisdictions.

The enabling nature of the legislation had created a framework for preservation by local option. The legislation had thereby eliminated the laborious local amendment process, which many viewed as an unnecessary stumbling block to local home rule.

Perhaps of greater importance was that both the legislature—through passage of the act—and a growing segment of the state's citizens—by expressing their opinion to legislators—had gone "on record" as favoring the development of meaningful local historic preservation programs. Also important was the fact that preservationists, contrary to popular opinion, were willing to compromise—by accepting exemptions of application—in an effort to further the progress of preservation within Georgia.

Effects of the Act

The net result of the passage of the Georgia Historic Preservation Act of 1980 was a strengthening of the concept of historic preservation within Georgia. The act created a mechanism that would encourage the development of a preservation dialogue between interested citizens and local elected officials.

Despite the limitations of the act—as represented by the compromise exemptions—Georgians for the first time had a framework for developing and implementing local preservation policy. The act gave greater meaning to other legislation, particularly the 1976 Facade and Conservation Easements Act. The 1976 statute provided for the granting of facade and conservation easements with subsequent tax benefits to those individuals granting said easements "to any governmental body or charitable or educational corporation, trust or organization which has the power to acquire interest in land," where such property was located within a locally designated historic district.

However, the problem with this legislation was its limited applicability—only a small number of locally designated historic districts existed in Georgia.[10] This limited number of districts reflected the absence of a state policy.

The Georgia Historic Preservation Act of 1980 filled this policy vacuum and further strengthened the 1976 statute by authorizing the acceptance of facade and conservation easements by local preservation commissions.

Passage of the 1980 act was only the first step in a new preservation era in Georgia. The next step was the development of public understanding of the legislative provisions and how these provisions could be used within local communities. Helping to develop that understanding is the purpose of this publication.

---

[1] Anthony R. Dees, "The Georgia Historical Society in Historic Preservation," *The Georgia Historical Quarterly* (Spring 1979).

[2] Philoclea Casey Eve, a kinswoman of Cunningham, was the first vice regent appointed by Cunningham. Eve served in that capacity from 1858 to 1889.

[3] For a detailed account of this important early preservation effort as well as an early history of the preservation movement, see Charles B. Hosner, *Presence of the Past: A history of the preservation movement in the United States before Williamsburg.* New York: G.P. Putnam's Sons, 1965.

[4] The term "War Between the States" is the traditional name in the South for what is also called the Civil War. The term is used here in recognition of the fact that historic preservation goes beyond objects to include place names and regional terms of reference.

[5] For a discussion of the role this property played in the development of national policy for DAR, see Hosner, *Presence of the Past.*

[6] Jann Haynes Gilmore, "Georgia's Historic Preservation Beginning: The Georgia Historical Commission (1951-1973)," *The Georgia Historical Quarterly* (Spring 1979).

[7] This initial conference was collectively sponsored by the Georgia Historical Commission, the Georgia Department of Archives and

History, the Georgia League of Historical Societies, the Georgia Conservancy, the Athens-Clarke Heritage Foundation, and The University of Georgia through its Institute of Community and Area Development (ICAD) and through the Georgia Center for Continuing Education.

[8] Brian McGreevy, Andrea Niles, Randy Jones, eds. *A Directory of Georgia Historical and Preservation Organizations,* The Georgia Trust for Historic Preservation, Atlanta, Ga., 1981, Pamphlet Series, no. 4.

[9] Developed by the author from information included in *A Directory of Georgia Historical and Preservation Organizations,* Georgia Trust, 1981.

[10] In recognition of this limitation, the 1976 Facade and Conservation Easements Act was amended in 1982 to include properties not within locally designated districts that were historically and architecturally significant and that had been designated as such by the State Historic Preservation Officer.

III
The Georgia Historic Preservation Act with Annotations

An Overview of the Act

Enacted by the General Assembly in 1980, the Georgia Historic Preservation Act (GHPA) establishes minimum standards for local jurisdiction protection of historic resources. In passing this legislation, it was generally believed that the General Assembly was addressing its constitutionally mandated responsibility for protecting vital areas and resources within Georgia.[1] Because of the manner in which the act was drafted, it offers communities a method of historic resource protection that is not tied to the exercise of zoning power.

Much of the municipal experience in historic resource protection within Georgia has been through the exercise of local zoning authority. However, since a majority of Georgia's local governments have not yet embraced the concept of zoning, the provision of an alternative protective method by the General Assembly was considered both appropriate and timely.

While establishing minimum standards,[2] the act reinforces the concept of home rule because only a local government can apply those standards. That application would be through the passage of an ordinance creating a local historic preservation commission. The passage of such an ordinance establishes local historic preservation policy as well as a means for implementing the policy.

As the agency responsible for policy implementation, the historic preservation commission recommends the designation of historic sites and districts; reviews proposals for all changes to designated properties; and approves or denies the proposals through a permit system.

The GHPA provides a benchmark against which each local governing jurisdiction may either evaluate existing preservation policy or formulate a preservation policy tailored to local needs.

The standards and procedures incorporated into the act reflect a local preservation policy that has been evolving since Charleston, South Carolina, created the nation's first municipally designated historic district in 1931. More than 800 communities across the nation have followed Charleston's example.

Of course, the success of local preservation policy depends upon citizen understanding and support. It is hoped that the following annotated review of the Georgia Historic Preservation Act will provide the necessary ingredients for citizen support of preservation policy wherever historic resources may exist in Georgia.

THE GEORGIA HISTORIC PRESERVATION ACT[3]
44-10-20 Short title
This Chapter shall be known and may be cited as the "Georgia Historic Preservation Act." (Ga. L. 1980, p. 1723, §1.) Effective April 8, 1980.

44-10-21 Legislative purpose; intent
The General Assembly finds that the historical, cultural, and aesthetic heritage of this state is among its most valued and important assets and that the preservation of this heritage is essential to the promotion of health, prosperity, and general welfare of the people.

Therefore, in order to stimulate the revitalization of central business districts in this state's municipalities;

to protect and enhance this state's historical and aesthetic attractions for tourists and visitors and thereby promote and stimulate business in this state's cities and counties;

to encourage the acquisition by cities and counties of facade and conservation easements pursuant to the "Facade and Conservation Easements Act of 1976"; and

to enhance the opportunities for federal tax relief of this state's property owners under the relevant provisions of the "Tax Reform Act of 1976" allowing tax deductions for rehabilitation of certified historic structures, the General Assembly establishes a uniform procedure for use by each county and municipality in the state in enacting ordinances providing for the protection, enhancement, perpetuation, and use of places, districts, sites, buildings, structures, and works of art having a special historical, cultural, or aesthetic interest or value. (Ga. L., 1980, p. 1723, §2.)

1. Annotation:
This section lists the legislative justification for the Georgia Historic Preservation Act (GHPA). The legislative purpose includes the promotion of economic benefits accruing from revitalization of central business districts, the promotion of tourism, and qualification of historic properties for local and federal tax benefits. The reference to the establishment of uniform procedures for the enactment of ordinances suggests that this legislative act should and could be used as a blueprint for local ordinances.

Local ordinances should be drafted to be able to withstand attacks on their legality. Attention should be directed toward a careful and complete recitation of purpose that clearly states the local jurisdiction's reasons for enacting a preservation ordinance. In addition, it is generally recommended that the purpose clause of a preservation ordinance cite all of a local jurisdiction's reasons for establishing a preservation commission.[4] Special note should be taken to insure that aesthetics does not appear to be the sole, or major, motivation of the ordinance. While an increasing number of courts recognize aesthetics as a justifiable purpose for preservation ordinances, the traditional court reaction to aesthetics as the major motivating factor has been negative.

The Tax Reform Act of 1976 allows federal income tax deductions for rehabilitating certified historic structures that are within locally designated historic districts or that are listed on the National Register of Historic Places. This act has been superceded by the Economic Recovery Tax Act of 1981.

Providing a legislative framework for tax relief under the Tax Reform Act of 1976 was a major consideration in the General Assembly's enactment of the GHPA. It was envisioned that local district designation could qualify properties for tax relief more quickly than could the time-consuming National Register nomination process.

44-10-22 Definitions
As used in this article, the terms:

(1) "Certificate of appropriateness" means a document evidencing approval by an historic preservation commission of a proposal to make a material change in the appearance of a designated historic property or of a structure, site, or work of art located within a designated historic district, which document must be obtained before such material change may be undertaken.

(2) "Commission" means an historic preservation commission

created or established pursuant to the provisions of codes 44-10-24.

(3) "Designation" means a decision by the local governing body of the municipality or county, wherein a property or district proposed for preservation is located, to designate such property or district as an "historic property" or as an "historic district" and thereafter prohibit all material changes in appearance of such property or within such district prior to the issuance of a certificate of appropriateness by the historic preservation commission.

(4) "Exterior architectural features" means the architectural style, general design, and general arrangement of the exterior of a building or other structure, including but not limited to the kind or texture of the building material, and the type and style of all windows, doors, signs, and other appurtenant architectural fixtures, features, details, or elements relative to the foregoing.

(5) "Historic district" means a geographically definable area, urban or rural, which contains structures, sites, works of art, or a combination thereof which:

(A) have special character or special historical or aesthetic interest or value;

(B) represent one or more periods or styles of architecture typical of one or more eras in the history of the municipality, county, State, or region; and

(C) cause such area, by reason of such factors, to constitute a visibly perceptible section of the municipality or county.

(6) "Historic preservation jurisdiction" in the case of a county means the unincorporated area of such county and in the case of a municipality such term means the area within the corporate limits of such municipality.

(7) "Historic property" means a structure, site, or work of art, including the adjacent areas necessary for the proper appreciation or use thereof, deemed worthy of preservation by reason of its value to the municipality, county, State, or region for one or more of the following reasons:

(A) it is an outstanding example of a structure representative of its era; or

(B) it is one of the few remaining examples of a past architectural style; or

(C) it is a place or structure associated with an event or person of historic or cultural significance to the municipality, county, State, or region; or

(D) it is a site of natural or aesthetic interest that is continuing to contribute to the cultural or historical development and heritage of the municipality, county, State, or region.

(8) "Local governing body" means the elected governing body or governing authority of any municipality or county of this State.

(9) "Material change in appearance" means a change that will affect only the exterior architectural features of an historic property or of any structure, site, or work of art within an historic district and may include any one or more of the following:

(A) A reconstruction or alteration of the size, shape, or facade of an historic property, including relocation of any doors or windows or removal or alteration of any architectural features, details, or elements;

(B) Demolition of an historic property;

(C) Commencement of excavation;

(D) A change in the location of advertising visible from the public way on any historic property; or

(E) The erection, alteration, restoration, or removal of any building or other structures within a designated historic district, including walls, fences, steps, and pavements, or other appurtenant features except exterior paint alterations.

(10) "Person" includes any natural person, corporation, or unincorporated association.

(Ga. L. 1980, p. 1723, §3.)

2. Annotation:

This section defines the language of the legislation and articulates the criteria for evaluating an historic district or historic property. Also of prime importance is the listing of those factors constituting a material change in appearance. The understanding of this section is basic to the successful interpretation and utilization of the act.

44-10-23 Exemptions

Cities or counties which, as of March 31, 1980, have adopted ordinances relative to planning and zoning for historic purposes, under authority granted by local constitutional amendment or by any other means, shall not be required to comply with the provisions of this Chapter.

3. Annotation:

Prior to passage of the GHPA, all local jurisdiction controls on historic resources were undertaken under the approved, or assumed, local zoning authority. The GHPA is not a zoning law; it is a general law enacted under the General Assembly's authority to protect Georgia's vital areas and resources.

The GHPA represents the law of the state with respect to local jurisdiction protection of historic resources. There is an ever-pres-

ent potential for challenging local ordinances as being invalid. Thus, caution would dictate that local jurisdiction enactment of historic preservation ordinances conform with the GHPA. Those laws not consistent with the GHPA run the risk of invalidation.

44-10-24 Historic preservation commission—*establishment of designation; number, eligibility, and terms of members.*

(a) The local governing body of a municipality or county electing to enact an ordinance to provide for the protection, enhancement, perpetuation, or use of historic properties or historic districts shall establish or designate an historic preservation commission. Such local governing body shall determine the number of members of the commission, which shall be at least three, and the length of their terms, which shall be no greater than three years. A majority of the members of any such commission shall have demonstrated special interest, experience, or education in history or architecture; all the members shall reside within the historic preservation jurisdiction of their respective municipality or county, except as otherwise provided by subsection (b) of this code section; and all shall serve without compensation. In establishing such a commission and making appointments to it, a local governing body may seek the advice of any State or local historical agency, society, or organization.

(b) The local governing body of a county and the local governing body or bodies of one or more municipalities lying wholly or partially within such county may establish or designate a joint historic preservation commission. If a joint commission is established, the local governing bodies of the county and municipality or municipalities involved shall determine the residence requirements for members of the joint commission. (Ga. L. 1980, p. 1723, §4.)

4. Annotation:

Establishment of an historic preservation commission is accomplished through the enactment of a local ordinance specifying the powers and duties of the commission as well as *the number of members, terms of appointment, residency requirements, etc. Subsequently, commission members survey and research historic properties within the local jurisdiction and recommend the designation of either sites or districts as historic properties.*

Care should be taken to insure that the ordinance provides for the designation of districts as well as individual landmarks, thus providing the opportunity to protect all historic resources within the local jurisdiction. Through the procedure specified in the GHPA, the commission recommends designation of properties and the local government enacts one or more ordinances to establish the designation of an historic district or landmark.

The classification of the GHPA as representative of minimum standards relates to two aspects of this section of the act: the number of commission members and the qualifications of members. The reason for drafting the act to reflect minimum standards—instead of a preferred optimum—was to be certain that the many smaller communities in Georgia could meet the requirements of the GHPA.

The ideal membership composition of a commission (beyond the minimum of three) would be no less than five and no more than eleven. An odd number of members minimizes the potential of tie votes. In establishing the number of members, the local governing body should recognize that too small a commission will be open to charges of individual bias, while too large a commission may become difficult to handle.[5]

Of course, the ultimate factor in establishing the number of commission members will be the number of citizens with the necessary qualifications. Typically, preservation ordinances specify that members have professional backgrounds to guarantee that the commission, as a body, will have the knowledge and experience to evaluate and decide matters coming before it. These professional background requirements supplement a demonstrated interest, knowledge, or education in architecture or history.

Many areas in Georgia do not have architects, attorneys, or other designated resident professionals interested in or knowledgeable about architecture or history. This possible situation is the reason why the minimum standard level of commission members' qualifications was incorporated into the GHPA.

The ideal professional background requirements of the minimum number of five commission members would be: (1) an architect, (2) an historian, (3) a real estate expert, (4) a landscape architect, and (5) an attorney. Note that all of these professionals should be required to meet the minimum standard requirements of demonstrated *special interest, experience, or education in the history or architecture of the local jurisdiction.*

44-10-25 Powers and duties

Any municipal, county, or joint historic preservation commission appointed or designated pursuant to code section 44-10-24 shall be authorized to:

(1) Prepare an inventory of all property within its respective historic preservation jurisdiction having the potential for designation as historic property;

5. Annotation:
The inventory should be a commission's first undertaking. It becomes the basis for local preservation policy implementation. The inventory may be accomplished with the assistance of volunteers, local organizations, or preservation professionals.[6] Preservation commissions should build upon the research that may already have been completed by local historic societies and preservation organizations as well as the State Historic Preservation Office.

In addition, commissions will want to be aware of local properties that have been the subject of National Register nominations or recorded by the Historic American Buildings Survey (HABS) or the Historic American Engineering Record (HAER). The preservation commission should develop a reciprocal working relationship with the State Historic Preservation Officer, as well as local preservation-related organizations, so that the sharing of research information on historic resources can benefit local, state, and national programs.

(2) Recommend to the municipal or county local governing body specific places, districts, sites, buildings, structures, or works of art to be designated by ordinances as historic properties or historic districts;

6. Annotation:
Based upon an inventory, the commission recommends the designation of historic properties to the local government. The commission serves local government in an advisory capacity with the local government making the final designation.

(3) Review applications for certificates of appropriateness and grant or deny same in accordance with the provisions of section 44-10-28;

(4) Recommend to the municipal or county local governing body that the designation of any place, district, site, building, structure, or work of art as an historic property or as an historic district be revoked or removed;

7. Annotation:
While it is seldom necessary to revoke a designation, there are occasions when the loss of significance, or actual destruction, of an historic property makes this course of action appropriate.

(5) Restore or preserve any historic properties acquired by the municipality or county;

(6) Promote the acquisition by the city or county governing authority of facade easements and conservation easements in ac-

cordance with the provisions of the "Facade and Conservation Easements Act of 1976" (code sections 44-10-1 through 44-10-5);

(7) Conduct an educational program on historic properties located within its historic preservation jurisdiction;

(8) Make such investigations and studies of matters relating to historic preservation as the local governing body or the commission itself may, from time to time, deem necessary or appropriate for the purposes of this Chapter;

(9) Seek out State and Federal funds for historic preservation and make recommendations to the local governing body concerning the most appropriate use of any funds acquired;

(10) Consult with historic preservation experts in the Historic Preservation Section of the Department of Natural Resources or its successor and the Georgia Trust for Historic Preservation, Inc.; and

(11) Submit to the Historic Preservation Section of the Department of Natural Resources or its successor a list of historic properties or historic districts designated as such pursuant to code section 44-10-26. (Ga. L. 1980, p. 1723, §5.)

8. Annotation:

The broad scope of powers provided by the GHPA insures maximum flexibility in the development and implementation of local preservation policy.

44-10-26 Designation by ordinance of historic properties or historic districts; required provisions; investigation and report; submitted to the Department of Natural Resources; notice and hearing; notification of owners.

(a) Ordinances designating historic properties or historic districts adopted by local governing bodies shall be subject to the following requirements:

(1) Any ordinance designating any property as historic property or any district as an historic district shall require that the designated property or district be shown on the official zoning map of the county or municipality adopting such ordinance or, in the absence of an official zoning map, that it be shown on a map of the county or municipality adopting such ordinance and kept by the county or municipality as a public record to provide notice of such designation in addition to other notice requirements specified by this code section;

9. Annotation:

The purpose of this requirement is to prevent the possibility of an individual unknowingly purchasing a designated historic property subject to review by a preservation commission. This requirement is consistent with the emphasis the GHPA places on public knowledge, notification, and involvement regarding the historic designation process.

Another benefit of a public record of historic property designation is the usefulness of such record to other local governmental agencies that will want to consider the preservation commission's expertise before making their own decisions.

If experience in other parts of our nation is any indication, it is unlikely that an individual would unknowingly purchase a locally designated historic property. Realtors have learned that the historic designation enhances the appeal and value of property; thus, the historic significance of a property is a favorable sales factor. In addition, local historic designation, which includes a design review requirement, is recognized nationwide as a factor that stabilizes neighborhoods, protects property investments, and appreciates the value of property.

(2) Any ordinance designating any property as historic property shall describe each property to be designated, shall set forth the name or names of the owner or owners of the property, and shall require that a certificate of appropriateness be obtained from the historic preservation commission prior to any material change in appearance of the designated property; and

(3) Any ordinance designating any district as an historic district shall include a description of the boundaries of such district, shall list each property located therein, shall set forth the name or names of the owner or owners of each such property, and shall require that a certificate of appropriateness be obtained from the historic preservation commission prior to any material change in appearance of any structure, site, or work of art located within the designated historic district.

10. Annotation:

Designation of properties involves making a distinction between historic properties and historic districts. There is a need for the local ordinance to provide for the designation of both categories of historic resources.

Traditionally, local ordinances have been of two types: landmark ordinances and historic district ordinances. Although both of these ordinance types are concerned with the preservation of structures through design review, there is a difference in the scope and authority of the two approaches.

An historic district ordinance controls a specific area, or district, in which a majority of structures are of architectural or historic significance. By comparison, a landmark ordinance covers an entire city or county. The buildings protected are individual structures randomly located within the area of jurisdiction.

The GHPA combines these two approaches by providing for the designation of landmarks, or historic properties, as well as districts. Obviously, the location of historic resources within a community, or other area of jurisdiction, will determine whether there are one or more districts and/or landmarks designated.

(b) No ordinance designating any property as an historic property, and no ordinance designating any district as an historic district, nor any amendments thereto, may be adopted by the local governing body, nor may any property be accepted or acquired as historic property by said local governing body, until the following procedural steps have been taken:

(1) The commission shall make or cause to be made an investigation and shall report on the historic, cultural, architectural, or aesthetic significance of each place, district, site, building, structure, or work of art proposed for designation or acquisition. This report shall be submitted to the Historic Preservation Section of the Department of Natural Resources or its successor which will be allowed 30 days to prepare written comments concerning the report;

11. Annotation:

This report serves as a justification for the commission's recommendation for historic designation. Submission of the report to the Historic Preservation Section provides the opportunity for a professional review and subsequent articulation of the significance of the subject property.

(2) The commission and the local governing body shall hold a public hearing on the proposed ordinance. Notice of the hearing shall be published at least three times in the principal newspaper of general circulation within the municipality or county in which the property or properties to be designated or acquired are located; and written notice of the hearing shall be mailed by the commission to all owners and occupants of such properties. All the notices shall be published or mailed not less than 10 nor more than 20 days before the date set for the public hearing; and

12. Annotation:

The involvement of the public, and particularly those property

owners who would be affected, is clearly a central aspect of the historic designation process. Much of the opposition to the designation of historic properties by local preservation commissions seems to be founded upon the fear of arbitrary designation of properties.

This legislation seeks to address that fear by: (1) requiring an investigative report evaluating the significance of the property; (2) providing the opportunity for a professional review of the investigative report by a state agency; (3) requiring public notice; (4) providing for public hearings; and (5) providing that the actual designation be made by the local governing body instead of the preservation commission.

Thus, there is a very deliberate procedure that negates the possibility of arbitrary designation and definitely places the process in the arena of public business, where democratic procedures and majority opinion are the basis for action.

(3) Following the public hearing, the local governing body may adopt the ordinance as prepared, adopt the ordinance with any amendments it deems necessary, or reject the proposal.

(c) Within 30 days immediately following the adoption of the ordinance, the owners and occupants of each designated historic property and the owners and occupants of each structure, site, or work of art located within a designated historic district shall be given written notification of such designation by the local governing body, which notice shall apprise said owners and occupants of the necessity for obtaining a certificate of appropriateness prior to undertaking any material change in the appearance of the historic property designated or within the historic district designated. (Ga. L. 1980, p. 1723, §6.)

13. Annotation:

In addition to notification of the necessity of obtaining a certificate of appropriateness, notice also should be provided for the application procedure and the design guidelines used by the commission. Design guidelines are the criteria developed by commissions to evaluate proposed changes or additions to designated properties. The guidelines inform property owners how their applications will be judged. These guidelines are also useful in educating the public about the character of sites and/or districts and how to protect that character.

Other benefits of design guidelines can be: (1) provision—to the commission—of minimum standards for making decisions; (2) assurance that all applicants are treated uniformly and fairly;

(3) promotion of consistency in decisions; (4) clarification of standards of appropriateness for applicants, architects, and contractors, making it easier for them to comply; and (5) education of property owners about rehabilitation and maintenance techniques that will retain architectural integrity and enhance property value.

Generally, design guidelines fall into three categories: (1) rehabilitation and maintenance of existing structures; (2) new construction, either as additions to existing buildings or new structures on vacant land; and (3) environmental features such as signs, walls, fences, sidewalks, outdoor lighting, landscape, etc.

While it is easy to generalize about categories of design guidelines, the characters of individual historic properties and historic districts are actually very different from one another. Therefore, care should be taken to insure that guidelines developed reflect the distinctive character of a community and/or that of individual districts.

No commission should copy the guidelines developed for another community without checking to determine whether the two areas are similar enough for the same guidelines to work effectively. For information on the development of local design guidelines, consult Design Review in Historic Districts: A Handbook for Virginia Review Boards *by Alice Meriwether Bowsher.*

44-10-27 Certificate of appropriateness—when required; local or state actions

(a) After the designation by ordinance of an historic property or of an historic district, no material change in the appearance of such historic property or of a structure, site, or work of art within such historic district shall be made or be permitted to be made by the owner or occupant thereof unless and until application for a certificate of appropriateness has been submitted to and approved by the commission. Such application shall be accompanied by such drawings, photographs, or plans as may be required by the commission.

14. Annotation:

The fundamental provision of a preservation ordinance is the requirement that the preservation commission review and approve proposed changes to existing structures within a designated district, or to a designated historic property (landmark). The GHPA provides for control over "material change in appearance," which is defined in the act's section on definitions.

Application for a certificate of appropriateness should include plans, drawings, a description of materials, and other details giving the commission full knowledge of the proposed changes. In addition, the applicant should provide information indicating the relationship of the proposed work to adjacent buildings. The scope of the work proposed will dictate the information needed by the commission.

Certificates of appropriateness are required for all changes, as defined by the GHPA, whether or not a building permit is required. In instances requiring a building permit, the permit is issued only after the applicant has obtained a certificate of appropriateness.

(b) The Department of Transportation (DOT) and any contractors, including cities and counties, performing work funded by DOT are exempt from this article. Local governments are exempt from the requirement of obtaining certificates of appropriateness; provided, however, that local governments shall notify the commission 45 days prior to beginning an undertaking that would otherwise require a certificate of appropriateness and allow the commission an opportunity to comment.
(Ga. L. 1980, p. 1723, §7.)

15. Annotation:

A realistic assessment of the limitation, imposed by exemptions, of the GHPA will include the following factors:

(1) The GHPA exemption of DOT does not exempt DOT from responsibility for consideration of historic properties listed (or eligible for listing) on the National Register. Under the National Historic Preservation Act, using federal funds for any highway department project necessitates an environmental review to assess any potential negative impact on an historic property;
(2) The provision of the opportunity for a local commission to comment on local government activities will mitigate possible negative actions, especially since elected officials and the general populace will have demonstrated a concern for the protection of historic resources by virtue of the support for, and creation of, a local preservation commission.

44-10-28 Review of applications; procedure; approval, modification, or rejection; negotiations for acquisitions; variances; appeals.
(a) Prior to reviewing an application for a certificate of appropriateness, the commission shall take such action as may reasonably

be required to inform the owners of any property likely to be affected materially by the application and shall give the applicant and such owners an opportunity to be heard. In cases where the commission deems it necessary, it may hold a public hearing concerning the application.

(b) The commission shall approve the application and issue a certificate of appropriateness if it finds that the proposed material change in appearance would not have a substantial adverse effect on the aesthetic, historical, or architectural significance and value of the historic property or the historic district.

In making this determination, the commission shall consider, in addition to any other pertinent factors, the historical and architectural value and significance, architectural style, general design, arrangement, texture, and material of the architectural features involved and the relationship thereof to the exterior architectural style and pertinent features of other structures in the immediate neighborhood.

16. Annotation:

A preservation commission serves as trustee to insure the continued integrity of an historic property or district. The work of the commission in the approval and/or denial of certificates of appropriateness affecting districts and individual properties should be conducted as a meeting open to the public. In most instances, the applicant will be the only person interested in speaking on a particular application.

However, the commission should always be prepared to offer application opponents the opportunity to address the commission. To this end, many commissions choose to leave the record of their public meeting open for a few days after the meeting in order to receive written submissions for inclusion as a part of their records.

(c) In its review of applications for certificates of appropriateness, the commission shall not consider interior arrangements or uses having no effect on exterior architectural features.

17. Annotation:

Many individuals confuse the authority of preservation commission ordinances with land use zoning ordinances. As indicated previously, the preservation commission authority is related to exterior appearance only and not to interior arrangement or use of a structure.

Land use zoning, on the other hand, regulates the use of property and not appearance. In communities that have adopted historic zoning, this "appearance" authority is a separate authority and is exercised in addition to land use zoning.

(d) The commission shall approve or reject an application for a certificate of appropriateness within not more than 45 days after the filing thereof by the owner or occupant of an historic property or a structure, site, or work of art located within an historic district. Evidence of approval shall be by certificate of appropriateness issued by the commission. Failure of the commission to act within said 45 days shall constitute approval, and no other evidence of approval shall be needed.

(e) In the event the commission rejects an application, it shall state its reasons for doing so and shall transmit a written record of such action and reasons therefore to the applicant. The commission may suggest alternative courses of action it thinks proper if it disapproves the submitted application. If he or she so desires, the applicant may make modifications to the plans and may resubmit the application at any time after doing so.

18. Annotation:

One practice used by commissions interested in minimizing application rejections is adopting a pre-application review procedure designed to warn applicants of probable commission disapproval of an application not yet formally submitted.

(f) In cases where the application covers a material change in a structure's appearance that would require the issuance of a building permit, the commission's rejection of an application for a certificate of appropriateness shall be binding upon the building inspector or other administrative officer charged with issuing building permits. In such a case, no building permit shall be issued.

(g) Where such action is authorized by the local governing body and is reasonably necessary or appropriate for the preservation of a unique historic property, the commission may enter into negotiations with the owner for the acquisition by gift, purchase, exchange, or otherwise of the property or any interest therein.

19. Annotation:

This provision provides the mechanism for both federal and local tax relief to individuals willing to donate facade easements to the commission. For federal tax relief, the property must be listed on the National Register. To qualify for local tax benefits, the property must be listed on the National Register or be an historic property as designated by the local commission in compliance with the Georgia Facade and Conservation Easements Act of 1976, as amended in 1982.

*Where a commission's authority does not include a permanent
ban on demolition and, instead, is limited to a stay of demolition,
this provision can be a measure of last resort through which the
local jurisdiction, itself, can negotiate with the property owner to
prevent demolition of the designated property.*

(h) Where, by reason of unusual circumstances, the strict application of any provision of this Chapter would result in exceptional
practical difficulty or undue hardship upon any owner of any
specific property, the commission in passing upon applications
shall have power to vary or modify strict adherence to said provisions or to interpret the meaning of said provisions so as to relieve
such difficulty or hardship: Provided, however, that such variance,
modification, or interpretation shall remain in harmony with the
general purpose and intent of said provisions so that the architectural or historical integrity or character of the property shall be
conserved and substantial justice done. In granting variations, the
commission may impose such reasonable and additional stipulations and conditions as will, in its judgment, best fulfill the purpose
of this article.

(i) The commission shall keep a record of all applications for
certificates of appropriateness and of all its proceedings.

(j) Any person adversely affected by any determination made by
the commission relative to the issuance or denial of a certificate of
appropriateness may appeal such determination to the governing
body of the county or municipality in whose historic preservation
jurisdiction the property in question is located; and such governing
body may approve, modify, and approve or reject the determination made by the commission if the governing body finds that the
commission abused its discretion in reaching its decision.

The ordinances adopted in conformity with code section 44-10-26
shall specify the procedures for the review of decisions of the
commission by the governing body of the county or municipality
involved. Appeals from decisions of said governing body made
pursuant to this article may be taken to the superior court in the
manner provided by law for appeals from conviction for municipal
or county ordinance violations.

(Ga. L. 1980, p. 1723, §8.)

44-10-29 *Certain changes or uses not prohibited*
Nothing in this article shall be construed to prevent the ordinary
maintenance or repair of any exterior architectural feature in or on
an historic property when maintenance or repair does not involve a
material change in design, material, or outer appearance thereof,

nor to prevent any property owner from making use of this property not prohibited by other laws, statutes, ordinances, or regulations. (Ga. L. 1980, p. 1723, §9.)

44-10-30 Violations of this article, penalties.

Violations of any provision of an ordinance adopted in conformity with this article shall be punished in the same manner as provided by charter or local law for the punishment of violations of other validly enacted municipal or county ordinances. (Ga. L. 1980, p. 1723, §10.)

20. Annotation:

There is always concern that penalties for ordinance violations be strong enough to deter potential violators and yet not so strong that the ordinance is unlikely to be enforced. In Georgia, these violations are classified as misdemeanors and the fines are not likely to be large. Many ordinances, nationwide, combat the weakness of relatively small fines by considering each day of violation as a separate offense punishable by fine.

44-10-31 Court action or proceedings to prevent improper changes or illegal acts or conduct.

The municipal or county local governing body or the historic preservation commission shall be authorized to institute any appropriate action or proceeding in a court of competent jurisdiction to prevent any material change in appearance of a designated historic property or historic district, except those changes made in compliance with the provisions of an ordinance adopted in conformity with this article, or to prevent any illegal act of conduct with respect to such historic property or historic district. (Ga. L. 1980, p. 1723, §11.)

---

[1] 1983 Georgia Constitution, Article III, Section VI, paragraph II, a 1: "Without limitation of the powers granted under paragraph I, the General Assembly shall have the power to provide by law for restrictions upon land use in order to protect and preserve the natural resources, environment, and vital areas of the state."

[2] It should be noted that local authority may provide for higher standards of preservation policy and compliance than those included in the act.

[3] Official Code of Georgia Annotated, Title 44; Chapter 10, "Historic Preservation"; Article 2, "Ordinances Providing for Historical Preservation," 1982.

[4]Stephen N. Dennis, *Recommended Model Provisions for a Preservation Ordinance with Annotations* (Washington, D.C.: National Trust for Historic Preservation, 1980).

[5]Ibid.

[6]Anne Derry, et al., *Guidelines for Local Surveys: A Basis for Preservation Planning* (Washington, D.C.: U.S. Department of the Interior, 1977).

IV
Using the Georgia Historic Preservation Act in Your Community

With the passage of the Georgia Historic Preservation Act (GHPA), Georgians were given guidelines, if not actual directions, for creating local preservation policy. However, advocates faced an uphill battle in communities where residents had never given thought to creating such a policy. The difficulty was—and all too often still is—one of informing people of what they have, why it is important, how it is endangered (because its value is not recognized), how it can be protected, and who should be involved in that protection. Quite simply, the battle involves conducting a community education program that will engineer the consent necessary for a local government to establish a preservation policy.

The Engineering of Consent

Each city and county government will decide individually whether to use the GHPA. Basic to that decision will be the degree of local concern for protection of historic resources as well as a belief that government can and should have a role in that protection. The exact nature of a local government's role in historic resource protection will depend upon citizen understanding of the potential benefits of a preservation commission.

But how do you introduce the concept of historic resource protection within your community? The introduction usually begins with several individuals who recognize the value of protection and accept responsibility for initiating an educational program for both citizens and elected officials.

The exact nature of a community-oriented educational program in historic resource protection will vary from place to place. This variation occurs because such programs should meet local needs while they assure effective communication of resource concerns, problem areas, and potentials.

Although word-of-mouth can be an effective form of communication, conducting an organized, formal education program means less chance of distortion and misunderstanding. In addition, such a program provides the opportunity to structure the educational material in a logical sequence, allowing people to comprehend fully all aspects of the subject.

Given the resident expertise in educational program development found in many communities, as well as the host of organizations and agencies geared to community assistance, there is no reason that any community in Georgia could not develop an educational program on historic resource protection.[1]

Sponsorship

Those who organize a community educational program for historic resource protection will want to consider the benefits of soliciting community sponsors for the program. Appropriate sponsors would be the mayor and council, the county commissioners, civic clubs, community improvement groups, historic societies, youth organizations, senior citizen groups, and other special interest groups.

These sponsors will provide a collective endorsement and an immediate identification with the program for members of the sponsoring organizations, groups, and agencies. If the arrangement is appropriate, a representative of each sponsoring unit could serve as a member of a steering committee responsible for publicizing the program and soliciting citizen participation. The effectiveness of the entire program will depend upon the degree of community participation.

Designing a Program

People interested in developing educational programs on historic resource protection should consider five fundamental questions: (1) What do we have of historic significance? (2) Why are these resources important? (3) Do these resources need protection and, if so, in what ways are they threatened? (4) How have others protected historic resources and will those methods work in our area? and (5) What shall we do to protect the historic resources of our area?

The Process

In addressing these questions, the community can be guided through five associated phases: (1) discovery, (2) evaluation, (3) assessment, (4) investigation, and (5) decision-making.

Discovery

Discovery is an awareness phase in which various historic sites, structures, buildings, districts, and objects are identified and researched in terms of their historic, architectural, environmental, and cultural significance to the area. During this phase, people can learn basic terms describing building elements and learn how to identify building styles. Known as the development of visual literacy, this process will benefit all age groups within the community, including elementary school students.

Evaluation

Evaluation focuses upon the ways in which those historic resources identified in the discovery phase contribute to the community. In this phase, various benefits—both to individuals and to the community at large—are identified in terms of social, cultural, economic, and aesthetic values.

These benefits contribute to, and often determine, both the environmental quality of an area and the quality of life available to area residents. This information answers the question of why a resource is important and tells how preserving it can contribute to a community's health and well-being.

Assessment

Based upon the conclusions of the evaluation phase, the next step is assessing the current and projected physical condition of historic resources while considering any trends, policies, or practices that would endanger the survival of these resources. In so doing, we both answer the question of whether resources need protection and document the ways in which they are threatened. We thus determine the need for historic resource protection.

Investigation

Next, we consider how historic resources can be protected. At this point, it is helpful to investigate the ways in which other communities have approached this problem as well as the degree to which they have been successful. In the context of reviewing protective measures, the Georgia Historic Preservation Act can be studied for information about how a local preservation commission would be created, how it would operate, and how it could benefit the community.

Decision-making, the Final Phase

At this point, the community should be ready to enter the fifth and final phase: decision-making. This phase has three levels, each one represented by a question. Resolution of subquestions can answer these three questions. An affirmative answer to each level serves as the foundation for the consideration of the subsequent question. Negative responses require reconsideration and review of previous program material.

Level 1: Should historic resources be protected?
 Subquestions:
 a-Are historic resources of value to the community?
 b-What is the alternative to historic resource protection?

Comment:
 The value of historic resources can be expressed in terms of economics, energy, aesthetics, the environment, and history. Often, the historic resources of an area create its unique sense of place, which in turn provides a sense of identity to the individual and to the entire community.
 The alternative to protection of historic resources is a lack of protection. To accept lack of protection is to gamble with the future of other irreplaceable resources.

Level 2: Should the protection of historic resources be a policy of local government?
 Subquestions:
 a-What other means for protection are available?
 b-Can other means be as effective as local government?
 c-Is local government willing to protect historic resources?

Comment:
 Within the private sector of our society, numerous individuals and private organizations have developed historic resource protection programs. These programs have included such activities as implementing architectural surveys, establishing revolving funds for the purchase of endangered buildings, developing community education programs, and acquiring easements.
 While they may enjoy such success, these programs require an enormous ongoing commitment of time and money. When the commitment depends on volunteers, it is often difficult to sustain. These private programs are created, usually, in the absence of municipal policy. The success of private programs can never match the impact of local government policy.
 The willingness of local government to participate in historic

resource protection usually depends upon citizen understanding and support. With adequate support and encouragement from the electorate, few local officials hestitate to follow the example established by Charleston, South Carolina (see Chap. I, p. 4).

Since Charleston established an historic resource protection policy in 1931, more than 800 communities have followed that city's lead, thus providing even more evidence of the soundness of the concept.

Level 3: What should be the exact nature of historic resource protection within our community or area?

Subquestions:

a-How do we deal with the question of demolition?

b-What about the design character of new construction within an historic district?

c-Should we allow condemnation by neglect?

Comment:

Resolving these issues will determine local preservation policy. No single set of answers can be applied uniformly to every community or area. Instead, each community must examine its own resources and determine the extent to which these resources should be protected. Thus, in keeping with the American tradition of self-determination, each community will establish its own definition of historic preservation.

The demolition issue causes the greatest number of problems for preservation commissions. The loss of a building is not only irreversible, it is contrary to a commission's function—to protect the special character of historic districts.

Although the GHPA defines demolition as a material change in appearance that preservation commissions must review—and can deny—the development of demolition policy has been left to the individual community. Generally, a community follows one of two policies relating to demolition: (1) the commission has the right to deny demolition, or (2) the commission has the right to delay demolition.

The community with a strong preservation ordinance allows demolition requests to be denied. Weaker ordinances permit delaying demolition for varying periods of time. Obviously, a commission with the power to deny demolition will be far more successful in maintaining the character of historic structures and districts.

To assure objectivity in considering an application for demolition, the commission should have carefully drafted criteria with which to evaluate the request. These criteria may be specified in the ordinance or included in the commission's design guidelines.[2]

Another consideration about demolition is the requirement that a property owner have and present, as a part of the application for demolition, definite plans for the building that will replace the structure to be demolished. Otherwise, a commission could find itself a partner in site clearance that serves only to diminish an area's existing architectural character.

One major decision about local preservation policy concerns new construction within historic districts. Though few preservation commissions have to deal with the issue of new construction, the issue can be raised. Having an established policy is wise.

A common misconception is the belief that new construction is banned in historic districts. New construction is often encouraged when it is appropriate—however, it should not be used as an excuse to demolish existing structures that contribute to a district's character. The major question regarding new construction has to do with its design character and whether to allow contemporary or traditional design.

Arguments for contemporary design include promoting the idea of a continually evolving, living city with new buildings designed to be both expressive of their time and compatible with the existing historic architecture. When the untrained eye cannot distinguish between old and new, reproducing architectural styles is seen as freezing an area in time and destroying the value of historic structures. It is also argued that applying historic styles to contemporary supermarkets, laundromats, and service stations can reach the point of absurdity.

Supporters of traditional design question the appropriateness of contemporary design in an area dominated by historic styles of architecture. They feel that using traditional design styles is the best way to protect the historic character of an area.

In comparing these two points of view, architects may view policies encouraging contemporary architecture as unrestrictive while viewing traditional architecture requirements as unfair and restrictive.

Beyond the concern for the architectural character of proposed new construction is the need to consider building density, the historic pattern of building placement on the lot (set-

back), and the average amount of open space separating buildings. If new construction between existing structures is encouraged, the environmental character and physical appearance of an historic district could be destroyed.

A third issue worthy of consideration is condemnation by
neglect. Condemnation by neglect can be a deliberate or acci-
dental process whereby a property owner simply allows a
structure to deteriorate beyond a point of repair. This deterioration can be a strategy for eliminating the need to secure a
demolition permit or for circumventing the authority of a preservation commission.

Unless the preservation ordinance includes a specific prohi-
bition against condemnation by neglect, a community may find
itself losing a valuable part of its historic character because of
one person's decision. Health, safety, and building codes establish minimum standards of maintenance. Identifying standards,
by which minimum maintenance can be defined in the preservation ordinance, should establish local government authority for
preventing condemnation by neglect within historic districts.[3]

Evaluating the Process

Completing the decision-making process as a part of a community educational program should indicate support for creating a
local historic preservation commission.

Is this support drawn from a broad spectrum of the community?
Does this support include local government officials?

If not, or if participation in the program has not been widespread,
repeating the community education program may be necessary.
However, before repeating the program, ask citizens who have
already participated to evaluate the original program and make
suggestions for improving its educational effectiveness. When
these supporters are ready to present the program again, they
should undertake a special recruitment effort to solicit the participation of those who missed the initial program series.

Whether or not the historic resource protection supporters re-
peat the community education program, they should still give
special consideration to members of the local governing body. This
consideration should be in the form of a special program of review,
including: goals of the community education programs, issues related to historic resource protection, basic provisions of the GHPA,
potential benefits of a local preservation commission, and the
degree of local support for the creation of a preservation committee.

In addition to providing a program review for the governing body, this presentation will give the members an opportunity to ask questions. Essential to this presentation is a review of the process of creating a local preservation commission, with emphasis upon the two distinct phases of this creation.

Creating a Preservation Committee

In Phase I, the local governing body enacts an ordinance creating a preservation commission in accordance with the GHPA. However, without Phase II, the preservation commission is—in effect—a study committee empowered only to initiate a local historic resources survey; to develop the necessary mechanisms for operating an historic resource protection program; and to make recommendations for historic designations.

Nothing really becomes operational until the local governing body initiates Phase II through the passage of one or more additional ordinances designating specific sites and/or districts as historic properties. Thus, the local governing body retains full control of the local historic resource protection process.

This meeting with members of the local governing body is an appropriate time to review the special concerns that the members should keep in mind when they consider the creation of a preservation commission: (1) the caliber of appointees to a commission, and (2) the degree and nature of local government administrative support.

Paramount to the success of a commission will be the individuals appointed to implement its work. The best guarantee of success will be choosing highly motivated individuals meeting the qualifications required for appointment (see annotation 44-10-24 - Chap. III, p. 25).

The next critical factor for the commission's success will be the staff support provided by local government. Members of a commission are essentially volunteers serving without compensation.

Clerical staff members are necessary for such commission operations as correspondence, public information, receipt of applications for certificates of appropriateness, preparation of meeting agendas, meeting notifications, and maintenance of all records.

When possible, an administrative staff person with training in preservation planning, architectural history, or architecture should be employed to assist the commission on a continuing basis, thus assuring administrative stability. Many communities meet this need by assigning a planning, zoning, or building department staff person to the commission on a part-time basis.

Clerical and administrative support is not the only issue of concern. Facilities also pose a problem. Where will those responsible for clerical and administrative functions be housed? Where will the commission meet to review applications for certificates of appropriateness?

A separate office would enhance the identity and efficiency of a commission, but it is possible to have the staff function in other departmental or agency offices. The major concern, however, is making appropriate space arrangements at an early stage so that the commission's functions are not impaired through a stepchild relationship to other departments or agencies.

A suitable conclusion for a special presentation to the local governing body would be an offer to extend the group's educational activities to include a public relations program. The program would be designed to inform citizens of the exact nature of the ordinance proposed by the governing body for the establishment of an historic preservation commission. Such a program could include public meetings, newspaper articles, radio and television interviews, information programs, and printed material.

One of the most effective types of printed material is the brochure or flyer designed for widespread distribution. For such a brochure, the question/answer approach, illustrated in Appendix H, is most appropriate.

The creation of an historic preservation commission is a milestone in the history of any community, but it is only the beginning of an effort to establish a local historic resource protection program. A preservation commission will necessarily take initial actions that include three basic areas: (1) the initiation of an historic resource survey, (2) the adoption of operational standards, and (3) the creation of a public information program.

Establishing a Protection Program

Conducting the Historic Resource Survey

The historic resource survey provides the documentary foundation for the commission's program. It identifies the historic character of a community or area and provides the basis for recommendations of historic site or district designation.

As defined by the National Register, an historic resource is a district, site, building, structure, or object that is significant in American history, architecture, archaeology, and culture. Thus, an historic resource may be a block of commercial buildings or the home of an early settler, a bridge or a city park, a railroad station or an Indian mound.

When we mention an historic resource survey, we are not talking about the traditional architectural survey that deals with only buildings and structures. Instead, if we are to identify districts, our concern is to inventory an area's visual and environmental character. It is the relationship of both natural and manmade features that provides the distinctive character and identity of an area. In New Orleans' Vieux Carre, for example, this concept is known as "tout ensemble" and is defined as the whole being of greater value than the individual parts.

In addition to the buildings and structures usually included in the architectural survey, the historic resource survey should include the major natural features that contribute to the identity of an area: the archaeological, historic, and cultural sites, as well as those aspects of the townscape that contribute to form and image. Thus, the historic resource survey is a combination of historic, visual, and physical factors that collectively determines the ambience of an area.[4]

What to include in an historic resource survey is only one consideration. Another is the question of how large an area the survey should cover.

It is recommended that the entire jurisdiction of the city or county be surveyed at one time, rather than pre-selecting one or more areas. The preferential surveying of one or more areas has a negative effect, both politically and psychologically, on residents of other areas within the jurisdiction.

Once the survey is completed, a number of factors will determine the priority of historic designation. However, the eligibility of areas, as determined by the survey, may itself help to safeguard valuable historic resources prior to actual designation.

Increasingly, communities are retaining preservation planners, as well as other planning and design professionals, to undertake historic resource surveys. Even when a community has volunteer assistance available, it is advisable to hire at least one professional who can develop the survey program, administer survey activities, coordinate the work being done, and make program decisions. Help in conducting such surveys may be obtained from the preservation agencies listed in Appendix I.

Adopting Operational Standards

The adoption of operational standards is the single most important aspect a newly created historic preservation commission undertakes. Operational standards can include two areas of concern: (1) rules of procedure, and (2) design guidelines.

Rules of procedure are the regulations, or bylaws, adopted by the commission for the administration of commission business. This business includes: (1) selecting officers and designating their duties; (2) conducting meetings, including setting up quorum requirements and developing a public record of the commission's meetings and decisions; and (3) establishing procedures for processing applications for certificates of appropriateness.

It is important that a commission adopt rules of procedure as soon as possible so that it will be able to function effectively and also to tell the public how it expects to conduct business. While it is possible for the basic ordinance to include rules of procedure, it is recommended that a commission be permitted to adopt its own rules of procedure so that it may retain the operating flexibility necessary to meet unexpected needs or demands. A suggested rules model is included in Appendix B.

Developing Design Guidelines

In developing design guidelines, the historic preservation commission establishes community standards for the care and protection of historic resources. Upon adoption by the commission, these standards are the objective criteria against which all proposals are evaluated.

Beauty, as the saying goes, is in the eye of the beholder. In the same way, far too often preservation commissions with no design guidelines find themselves in the undesirable position of making subjective decisions that brand them as arbiters of taste.

Design guidelines have several desirable functions, including the identification of important design review concerns, the promotion of objective and consistent decisions, and the reduction of the risks of court challenges.

The development of design guidelines should address four areas of concern: (1) rehabilitation and maintenance of existing buildings, (2) new construction, (3) signs, and (4) demolition and relocation. Each of the four areas represents a basic concern as well as related issues. The following outline presents those basic concerns and issues.

I. Rehabilitation and maintenance of existing buildings

The majority of applications to a preservation commission involves rehabilitating and maintaining existing buildings. A commission's basic concern in reviewing these applications is protecting and retaining as much of the original fabric as possible. This concern relates both to materials and design.

An excellent reference that identifies fundamental concepts and offers guidance for working with old buildings is *The Secretary of the Interior's Standards for Rehabilitation* and guidelines for application of those standards (see Appendix C).

The typical problem usually involves a conflict between the personal taste of an owner and the desirability of retaining historic authenticity. For example, an owner may propose to remove a Queen Anne verandah in an effort to create an older appearance, or propose to replace small paned windows with large paned windows to create a more modern appearance. In either case, the architectural integrity of the structure could be destroyed and, subsequently, the monetary value of the property could be significantly reduced.

Other problem areas include paint colors, synthetic siding, landscape character, and modern equipment. Paint colors probably generate the most disagreement. Some commissions regulate colors to prevent the disruptive effect of inappropriate colors. Other groups recognize that color can be changed easily and that its regulation is an issue that antagonizes many people.

Installing synthetic siding may involve removing architectural detail, a process that may change the appearance and destroy the architectural integrity of the building. When this is the case, a commission obviously would not be sympathetic to such a proposal. However, synthetic siding could be acceptable when it reproduces the dimensions of the original siding, as well as the relationship of corner boards, window molding, and other architectural details without changing the appearance of a building. Still debated are the functional advantages of synthetic siding, the validity of claims of low maintenance, and the effect of such siding on a building's structural integrity.[5]

There is a growing awareness of the landscape as an element of the historic fabric of a site or district. The subsequent concern for protecting historic landscape character recognizes the contribution of the landscape to an area's environmental quality. The protection of building settings and specific landscape elements, such as trees, can be incorporated into design guidelines for rehabilitation and maintenance.

Adding modern devices such as aluminum storm windows and doors, solar collectors, air conditioners, fire escapes, and television antennas can drastically alter the appearance of historic buildings.

Some commissions will approve storm windows and doors that are designed according to commission guidelines. Other commissions will allow air conditioners, fire escapes, etc., only when they cannot be viewed from the public right-of-way. Each commission needs to decide individually what to incorporate into its guidelines.

The key to sensitive rehabilitation and maintenance of existing buildings is educating the public about the significance of varying architectural styles and appropriate repair and maintenance technique. While a commission develops design guidelines to help the property owner in preparing applications for certificates of appropriateness, many communities have found the publication of a property owner's manual to be an excellent approach to the commission's community education needs. In addition to rehabilitation guidelines, the book can describe local architectural styles and repair and maintenance techniques for various building materials. One of the more complete property owner's manuals is *The Beaufort Preservation Manual,* prepared for the City of Beaufort, South Carolina, in 1979.[6] This publication discusses already mentioned aspects, along with weatherproofing and site improvements. Ultimately, these owner's manuals benefit the community at large. At the same time, they make the change-monitoring tasks of the preservation commission a more rewarding and satisfactory experience for all involved.

II. New construction

While new construction may not be a major problem in many historic districts, in certain instances it may be necessary or desirable. Developing guidelines for new construction in historic districts insures that the historic character of an area will be preserved by requiring design compatibility of new construction with existing buildings.

When one is considering the development of design guidelines for new construction, the basic issue is usually whether to encourage or discourage modern design. This decision will be based upon the community's concept of historic preservation and the degree to which the community is committed to the evolution of the physical city as a cultural continuum.

Beyond design form is the question of scale relationship between old and new buildings. Many sensitive designers are much more concerned with scale compatibility than with design compatibility. A contemporary high-rise building is so obviously a disruptive element in a typical 19th-century neighborhood that most preservation commissions include mandatory height limitations in new construction guidelines.

The 1960s' guidelines developed by Muldawer and Patterson for Savannah have subsequently served as inspiration for guidelines nationwide. Those using the Savannah information recognize the necessity of tailoring guidelines to reflect the unique character of the individual district to which they may be applied. Appendix D provides several examples of new construction guidelines. A major concern will be the effectiveness of guidelines. Effectiveness relates to a definition of compliance and the extent to which guidelines are mandatory. Savannah has 16 criteria, but only one—height—is mandatory, with the requirement that the designer meet any five of the remaining 15 criteria. Critics think these compliance criteria are too loose. Other communities have established much tighter control over new construction in historic districts.

III. Signs

Sign control has long been recognized as a tool for preventing visual chaos. Within an historic district, the control of signs assumes even greater importance. The basic concern is that signs in historic districts relate to the design elements of the building where the sign is located. Another important consideration is compatibility with the area's other signs and buildings in size, materials, color, typefaces, legibility, and placement. Although criteria for signs will vary from one community to another, the basic criteria included in Appendix E should be considered in the development of guidelines for signs.[7]

IV. Demolition and relocation

Once demolished, a building can never be replaced. The relocation of an historic building produces the same loss for an area. Should the building be moved to an area outside the historic district, the building will no longer be protected by the historic preservation ordinance. Whenever possible, building relocation should be resisted because a building loses its historic and environmental context in the relocation process. Also, if listed on the National Register, the building will be removed from the register, thus losing the recognition, protection, grant eligibility, and tax benefits accorded to national register properties.

Aside from retaining a building as a part of the historic fabric of an area, the basic concerns in evaluating a request for demolition or relocation are:

1. What is the contribution of the building to its immediate

surroundings and to the district as a whole?
2. What is the building's historic and architectural significance?
3. What is the structural condition of the building?
4. What redevelopment is planned for the demolition site and does this new development meet the guidelines for new construction in an historic district?
5. In the case of a relocation within an historic district, is the new site one on which the relocated building will be a harmonious addition to the existing neighborhood, or will it be incompatible with the surrounding structures?

These basic concerns suggest the need for criteria to evaluate demolition or relocation requests. Adopting such criteria will enable a commission to make objective determinations. Appendix F contains examples of demolition criteria developed by several commissions.

A Public Information Program

A common thread binding all commission efforts will be a concern for developing and maintaining public support for the commission and its program activities. This support must be sought within both the community at large and the structure of local government. Everyone must be made aware of: (1) What the commission is about—its purposes and programs; (2) Why the commission exists—the need and the value of its activities; (3) How the commission functions—its administrative structure and operational procedures; (4) When the commission meets—its calendar for meetings; and (5) Where and how the commission may be contacted—the location of its offices, the names and telephone numbers of commissioners.

In addition, the general public will need to know why individual sites or districts qualify for protection and what may be the particular significance of different properties or areas. There will also be the need to interpret various properties in the context of the community's history.

Publications and public meetings are the best vehicles for distributing information. A basic publication of the commission will be the preservation ordinance itself, along with brochures or pamphlets explaining the commission's operational procedures and design guidelines. Public meetings can include a program of presentations to various civic clubs, fraternal organizations, and other community groups. Slide talks that illustrate the heritage of an area as well as the concerns of the commission can be especially effective. With no public information officer, commission members may want to take turns making presentations to the community.

Another option is to recruit volunteers from the local citizen preservation organization, or historic society, to make public information presentations on behalf of the commission. In this time of shrinking budgets, nothing could be more appropriate than the joint development of a full-fledged public education program by the commission and local preservation-oriented groups and organizations. The commission should present itself as an agency willing to work with the community for the ultimate benefit of all concerned.

Since a commission exists at the pleasure of the mayor or manager and council and often depends upon other government officials to enforce its decisions, strong support within local government is essential—from the mayor and council and from administrative officials and staff. Communication is the key ingredient within local government, and keeping the channels of communication open is the major task. Perhaps the most important initiative of a newly organized preservation commission is the organization of workshops within local government. The function of these workshops could be to explain the basic purpose, goals, and organizational procedures of the commission as well as the ways in which others in government could help the commission in its endeavors. Those departments of local government most closely associated with the concerns of a local preservation commission are likely to be:

Planning department: As the agency responsible for comprehensive community development and enhancement, the relationship of the planning department to preservation concerns is obvious. There should be close cooperation and support between planning and preservation interests. Basic to this relationship is a clear recognition of the difference in the regulatory functions of the two agencies: planning department—land use; preservation commission—design review.

Building inspection department: The cooperation of this agency is essential for referral of projects requiring review, for proving that a certificate of appropriateness has been granted before issuing a building or demolition permit, and for the monitoring of compliance with commission decisions in the field. The understanding and cooperation of this city department is essential to the commission's design control responsibilities.

Fire marshal: This individual's interpretations can drastically affect efforts to retain the design integrity of 19th-century structures while meeting contemporary fire codes. The fire marshal deserves special attention. Experience has shown that in many communities the fire marshal's understanding and appreciating preservation concerns has resulted in the cooperative development of solutions that meet fire code needs without destroying the architectural integrity of the structure under consideration.

City engineering department: This agency is responsible for public improvement projects including lighting, underground utilities, street beautification, street and sidewalk paving. The engineering department is in a position to affect the physical character of an historic district. The preservation commission will want to establish a good working relationship with this agency.

City attorney: As the individual who will be involved in any legal challenges to the review decisions of a commission, the city attorney must be kept well informed about legal aspects of the commission's activities.

Both within government and within the community, understanding the commission's programs will depend upon an effective public information program. That understanding will provide the popular and political support necessary for the commission's operational effectiveness.

---

[1] See Appendix I for sources of assistance in educational program development.

[2] For examples of demolition criteria, see Appendix F.

[3] See Appendix G for three examples of minimum maintenance requirements.

[4] For a list of townscape elements which should be included in a survey, see James R. Cothran, et al., *Local History and Townscape Conservation: Opportunities for Georgia's Communities* (Atlanta, Ga.: Robert and Company, 1981). Also see Anne Derry, et al., *Guidelines for Local Surveys: A Basis for Preservation Planning* (Washington, D.C.: U.S. Department of the Interior, 1977).

[5] For additional information on the effect of synthetic siding on structural integrity, contact the Technical Preservation Services, Preservation Assistance Division, National Park Service, U.S. Department of the Interior, Washington, D.C. 20240.

[6] *The Beaufort Preservation Manual* (West Chester, Pa.: John Milner Associates, 1979).

[7]For a comprehensive reference to sign control, see William R. Ewald and Daniel R. Mandelker, *Street Graphics* (McLean, Va.: Landscape Architecture Foundation, 1971).

V
It's Your Community

The GHPA was developed as a set of minimum standards for the local protection of historic resources. It addresses itself to one of the vital areas of our state's environment, the physical manifestations of our heritage. It also reinforces the constitutionally mandated right of the state's political jurisdictions to control growth and development for the benefit of the citizenry.

Whether the historic resources symbolizing the heritage of a community or area are protected, used, preserved, or destroyed is not a matter for which any state agency or organization is responsible. That responsibility rests with each local government, which, as a body of elected officials, represents the desires of its constituency. In turn, the ultimate responsibility belongs to the individual citizens who have collectively elected their government officials.

As stated earlier, historic preservation is a concern that has emerged primarily since World War II. Many communities still do not consider preservation to be of consequence. If a problem, need, or opportunity is not recognized, it will not be addressed. An old adage describes the situation another way: the eye is blind to what the mind does not see. In many communities both citizens and elected officials must first identify the need and the opportunity for historic resource protection.

But who will do this? Only those individuals, groups, or organizations who recognize the value of historic resources and who will assume the responsibility of sharing this insight with others. This question of leadership is an all too prevalent problem in many communities. However, unless an individual, or group, is willing to provide the necessary leadership, the needs, problems, and opportunities for historic resource protection will never be recognized. Leadership in the protection of historic resources involves the processes of education and persuasion. Successive processes will create an ongoing cycle of education about the commission's activities. Concern and communication about the protection of historic resources are part of a continuous process of monitoring change within the built environment, a process in which every citizen has—or should have—a role.

The Role of Citizens

In the past, American society valued civic duty and the obligation of citizens to serve the community. Too often today there is little sense of civic duty and few ideas about the concept of citizenship. This condition has been linked to the sense of rootlessness that increasingly characterizes our mobile society. Some of the symptoms of rootlessness are a sense of alienation from others, an unwillingness to be involved in situations requiring responsibility to others, and a failure to identify with the physical environment. Thus, it is possible for individuals to move from place to place without ever developing a sense of belonging, a sense of involvement and participation, a sense of place. It is through a sense of place that individuals obtain part of their identity.

Webster defines a citizen as "an inhabitant of a city or town or, a native or naturalized person, who owes allegiance to a government and is entitled to reciprocal protection from it." In this definition, Webster recognizes residency as the basic condition of citizenship as well as the symbiotic relationship between citizens and government; i.e., each performs (or should perform) for the benefit of the other. Webster goes on to define citizenship as the status of being a citizen and the quality of an individual's response to membership in a community.

In ancient Athens, citizenship was highly prized and not lightly conferred. In fact, it required an oath of allegiance in which an individual promised to defend the city from its enemies, uphold its laws, and to "transmit this city not less, but greater, and more beautiful than it was transmitted to us."

The Athenian Oath represents a quality of citizenship worthy of emulation. It also represents a creed consistent with the intent of historic preservation commissions: to leave the city not lesser, but greater, and more beautiful than they find it. Like ancient Athens, modern communities need to interpret citizenship and civic duty in terms of the protection and enhancement of the physical aspects of the community, including historic resources.

When individuals can act collectively to achieve that end, physical change within a community will be in harmony with its surroundings, will add to citizens' quality of life, and will reinforce the sense of place. This is both the goal and the challenge of those who seek to develop community preservation programs.

Appendix A

A Model Preservation Ordinance

The following model has been developed for use by local governmental jurisdictions. As provided by the GHPA, cities, counties, or cities and counties jointly, may establish local preservation commissions. Where the term (jurisdiction) occurs, simply insert the name of the city or county establishing the ordinance. Note the several options included which present an opportunity to articulate local preservation policy.

HISTORIC PRESERVATION COMMISSION ORDINANCE

AN ORDINANCE TO ESTABLISH AN HISTORIC PRESERVATION COMMISSION IN THE (JURISDICTION); TO PROVIDE FOR DESIGNATION OF HISTORIC PROPERTIES OR HISTORIC DISTRICTS; TO PROVIDE FOR ISSUANCE OF CERTIFICATES OF APPROPRIATENESS; TO PROVIDE FOR AN APPEALS PROCEDURE; TO REPEAL CONFLICTING ORDINANCES; AND FOR OTHER PURPOSES.
BE IT ORDAINED BY THE (MAYOR AND COUNCIL OR COUNTY COMMISSIONERS) OF THE (JURISDICTION)

Section 1

Purpose

In support and furtherance of its findings and determination that the historical, cultural, and aesthetic heritage of the (jurisdiction) is among its most valued and important assets and that the preservation of this heritage is essential to the promotion of the health, prosperity and general welfare of the people;

In order to stimulate revitalization of the business districts and historic neighborhoods and to protect and enhance local historical and aesthetic attractions to tourists and thereby promote and stimulate business;

In order to enhance the opportunities for federal tax relief of property owners under relevant provisions of the Economic Recovery Tax Act of 1981 allowing tax investment credits for rehabilitation of certified historic structures (26 U.S.C.A., Section 191);

The (Mayor and Council/County Commissioners) of the (jurisdiction) hereby declare it to be the purpose and intent of this Ordinance to establish a uniform procedure for use in providing for the protection, enhancement, perpetuation, and use of places, districts, sites, buildings, structures, and works of art having a special historical, cultural, or aesthetic interest or value, in accordance with the provisions of the Ordinance.

Section II

Creation of an Historic Preservation Commission

A. *Creation of the Commission.*

The title of the Commission shall be the "(Jurisdiction) Historic Preservation Commission." Commission members shall be appointed by (jurisdiction) officials, and will have only advisory authority in recommending landmark and historic district designation.

B. *Commission Position within the (Jurisdiction) Government.*

"The (Jurisdiction) Historic Preservation Commission" shall be considered a part of the planning functions of the (jurisdiction).

C. *Commission Members: Number, Appointment, Terms, and Compensation.*

The Historic Preservation Commission shall consist of three (3) members appointed by the (Mayor/County Commission Chairman) and ratified by the (City Council/County Commission), who shall be residents of the (jurisdiction), who have demonstrated special interest, experience, or education in history, architecture, or the preservation of historic resources. Members shall serve three-year terms. Members may not serve more than two (2) consecutive terms. In order to achieve staggered terms, initial appointments shall be: one (1) member for one (1) year; one (1) member for two (2) years; and one (1) member for three (3) years. Members do not receive a salary, although they may be reimbursed for expenses.

OPTION:

The Historic Preservation Commission shall consist of five (5) members. Initial appointments shall be: two (2) members for one (1) year; two (2) members for two (2) years; and one (1) member for three (3) years.

D. *Statement of the Commission's Powers.*

The (Jurisdiction) Historic Preservation Commission shall be authorized to:

1. Prepare an inventory of all property within its respective historic preservation jurisdiction having the potential for designation as historic property;
2. Recommend to the (City Council/County Commission) specific places, districts, sites, buildings, structures, or works of art to be designated by ordinance as historic properties or historic districts;
3. Review applications for Certificates of Appropriateness, and grant or deny same in accordance with the provisions of this Ordinance;

4. Recommend to the (City Council/County Commission) that the designation of any place, district, site, building, structure, or work of art as an historic property or as an historic district be revoked or removed;
5. Restore or preserve any historic properties acquired by the (City/County);
6. Promote the acquisition by the (City/County) of facade easements and conservation easements in accordance with the provisions of the "Facade and Conservation Easements Act of 1976" (*Georgia Laws 1976*, p. 1181);
7. Conduct an educational program on historic properties located within its historic preservation jurisdiction;
8. Make such investigations and studies of matters relating to historic preservation as the local governing body or the Commission itself may, from time to time, deem necessary or appropriate for the purposes of preserving historic resources;
9. Seek out state and federal funds for historic preservation, and make recommendations to the (City/County) concerning the most appropriate uses of any funds acquired;
10. Submit to the Historic Preservation Section of the Department of Natural Resources a list of historic properties or historic districts designated;
11. Perform historic preservation activities as the official agency of (City/County) historic preservation program;
12. Employ persons, if necessary, to carry out the responsibilities of the Commission;
13. Receive donations, grants, funds, or gifts of historic property, and to acquire and sell historic properties. The Commission shall not obligate the (City/County) without prior consent;
14. Review and make comments to the State Historic Preservation Office concerning the nomination of properties within its jurisdiction to the National Register of Historic Places.

E. *Commission's Power to Adopt Rules of Procedure.*

The Commission shall adopt rules for the transaction of its business and consideration of applications; shall provide for the time and place of regular meetings, and for the calling of special meetings. The Commission shall have the flexibility to adopt rules of procedure without amendment to this Ordinance. A quorum shall consist of a majority of the members. The latest edition of *Roberts' Rules of Order* shall determine the order of business at all meetings.

F. *Commission's Authority to Receive Funding from Various Sources.*

The Commission shall have the authority to accept donations and shall insure that these funds do not displace appropriated governmental funds.

G. *Records of Commission Meetings.*

A public record shall be kept of the Commission's resolutions, proceedings, and actions.

Section III
Designation of Historic Districts and Landmarks

A. *Preliminary Research by the Commission.*

(1) Commission's Mandate to Conduct a Survey of Local Historical Resources: The Commission shall have the authority to compile and collect information and conduct surveys of historic resources within the (jurisdiction).

(2) Commission's Power to Recommend Districts and Buildings to (City Council/County Commission) for Designation: The Commission shall present to the (City Council/County Commission) nominations for historic districts and local landmarks.

(3) Preparation of a Report on Proposed Designations: The Commission shall prepare formal reports when nominating historic districts or local landmarks. These reports shall be used to educate the community and to provide a permanent record of the designation. The report will follow guidelines for nominating structures to the National Register of Historic Places (National Preservation Act of 1966), and shall consist of two (2) parts: a) a physical description, and b) a description of historic significance. This report will be submitted to the Historic Preservation Section of the Department of Natural Resources.

B. *Designation of an Historic District*

(1) Criteria for Selection of Historic Districts: An Historic District is a geographically definable area, which contains structures, sites, works of art, or a combination thereof, which:

a) have special character or special historic/aesthetic value or interest;

b) represent one or more periods or styles of architecture typical of one or more eras in the history of the municipality, county, state, or region;

c) cause such area, by reason of such factors, to constitute a visibly perceptible section of the municipality or county.

(2) Boundaries of an Historic District: Boundaries of an Historic District shall be specified on tax maps; these boundaries will be included in the separate ordinances designating local districts. Boundaries specified in legal notices shall coincide with the boundaries finally designated. Districts shall be shown on the Official Zoning Map or, in the absence of zoning, on an official map designated as a public record.

(3) Evaluation of Properties within Historic Districts: Individual properties within historic districts shall be classified as:
   a) Historic (more than 50 years old);
   b) Non-Historic (less than 50 years old, yet possessing architectural character);
   c) Intrusions (structures less than 50 years old which do not contribute to the historical character of the district).
(4) Affirmation of Existing Zoning: This Historic Preservation Ordinance is not a Use Ordinance, and local zoning laws, where they exist, remain in effect until modified.

C. *Designation of a Landmark.*

(1) Criteria for Selection of Landmarks: An historic landmark is a structure, site, work of art, including the adjacent area necessary for the proper appreciation or use thereof, deemed worthy of preservation by reason of value to the (jurisdiction), State of Georgia, or local region, for one or more of the following reasons:
   a) it is an outstanding example of a structure representative of its era;
   b) it is one of the few remaining examples of past architectural style;
   c) it is a place or structure associated with an event or person of historic or cultural significance to the (jurisdiction), State of Georgia, or the region.
(2) Boundary Description: Boundaries shall be clearly defined for individual properties on tax maps and located on the Official Zoning Map, or, in the absence of zoning, on an official map designated as a public record.

D. *General Matters Affecting Designation of Both Historic Districts and Landmarks.*

(1) Application for Designation of Historic District or Landmark:
   a) Historic District—An historical society, neighborhood association, or group of property owners may apply for designation.
   b) Landmark Structure—An historical society or property owner may apply for designation.
(2) Required Public Hearings: The Commission and the local governing body shall hold a Public Hearing on the proposed ordinance for designation. Notice of the hearing shall be published in at least three (3) consecutive issues in the legal organ of the (jurisdiction), and written notice of the hearing shall be mailed by the Commission to all owners and occupants of such properties. All such notices shall be published or mailed not less than ten (10) nor more than twenty (20) days prior to date set for the Public Hearing. A letter sent via the United States Mail

to the last-known owner of the property shall constitute legal notification under this Ordinance.

(3) Notification of Property Owners of Proposed Designation: Any ordinance designating any property or district as Historic shall describe each property to be designated, set forth the name(s) of the owner(s) of the designated property or properties, and require that a Certificate of Appropriateness be obtained from the Historic Preservation Commission prior to any material change in appearance of the designated property.

(4) Requirements Regarding District Boundaries: Any ordinance designating any property or district as Historic shall require that the designated property or district be shown on the Official Zoning Map, or other designated map in the absence of zoning, of the (jurisdiction) and kept as a public record to provide notice of such designation.

(5) Notification of Historic Preservation Section: Prior to designating any property or district as Historic, the Commission must submit a report on the historic, cultural, architectural, or aesthetic significance of each place, district, site, building/ structure, or work of art, to the Historic Preservation Section of the Department of Natural Resources; thirty (30) days will be allowed to prepare written comments.

(6) Ordinance for Designation Announcement: A decision to accept or deny the ordinance for designation shall be made within fifteen (15) days following the Public Hearing, and shall be in the form of a resolution to the (City Council/County Commission).

(7) Notification of Adoption of Ordinance for Designation: Within thirty (30) days immediately following the adoption of the ordinance for designation, the owners and occupants of each designated historic property, and the owners and occupants of each structure, site, or work of art located within a designated historic district shall be given written notification of such designation by the (City Council/County Commission); which notice shall apprise said owners and occupants of the necessity of obtaining a Certificate of Appropriateness prior to undertaking any material change in appearance of the historic property designated or within the historic district designated.

(8) Notification of Other Agencies Regarding Designation: The Commission shall notify all necessary agencies within the (jurisdiction) of the ordinance for designation, including the local historical organization.

(9) Moratorium on Applications for Alteration or Demolition while Ordinance for Designation is Pending: If an ordinance for designation is being considered, the Commission shall have the power to freeze the status of the involved property.

(10) Authority to Amend or Rescind Designation: The Commission

has the authority to amend and/or rescind the designation if necessary.

Section IV

Application to Preservation Commission for Certificate of Appropriateness

A. *Approval of Alterations or New Construction in Historic Districts or Involving Landmarks.*

After the designation by ordinance of an historic property or of an historic district, no material change in the appearance of such historic property, or of a structure, site, or work of art within such historic district, shall be made or be permitted to be made by the owner or occupant thereof, unless or until application for a Certificate of Appropriateness has been submitted to and approved by the Commission.

B. *Approval of New Construction within Designated Districts.*

The Commission shall issue Certificates of Appropriateness to new structures constructed within designated historic districts. These structures shall conform in design, scale, building materials, setback, and landscaping to the character of the district specified in the Commission's Design Guidelines.

C. *Guidelines and Criteria for Certificates of Appropriateness.*

When considering applications for Certificates of Appropriateness to existing buildings, the Secretary of the Interior's "Standards of Rehabilitation" shall be used as a guideline along with any other criteria adopted by the Commission.

D. *Submission of Plans to Commission.*

An application for Certificate of Appropriateness shall be accompanied by such drawings, photographs, or plans, as may be required by the Commission.

E. *Acceptable Commission Reaction to Application for Certificate of Appropriateness.*

(1) The Commission shall approve the Application and issue a Certificate of Appropriateness if it finds that the proposed material change(s) in the appearance would not have a substantial adverse effect on the aesthetic, historic, or architectural significance and value of the historic property or the historic district. In making this determination, the Commission shall consider, in addition to any other pertinent factors, the historical and architectural value and significance, architectural style, general design arrangement, texture, and material of the architectural

features involved, and the relationship thereof to the exterior architectural style, and pertinent features of the other structures in the immediate neighborhood.

(2) The Commission shall deny a Certificate of Appropriateness if it finds that the proposed material change(s) in appearance would have substantial adverse effects on the aesthetic, historic, or architectural significance and value of the historic property or the historic district.

F. *Public Hearings on Applications for Certificates of Appropriateness, Notices, and Right to be Heard.*

At least seven (7) days prior to review of a Certificate of Appropriateness, the Commission shall take such action as may reasonably be required to inform the owners of any property likely to be affected by reason of the application, and shall give applicant and such owners an opportunity to be heard. In cases where the Commission deems it necessary, it may hold a public hearing concerning the application.

G. *Interior Alterations.*

In its review of applications for Certificates of Appropriateness, the Commission shall not consider interior arrangement or use having no effect on exterior architectural features.

H. *Technical Advice.*

When dealing with difficult technical questions, the Commission shall have the power to seek expert advice.

I. *Deadline for Approval or Rejection of Application for Certificate of Appropriateness.*

(1) The Commission shall approve or reject an application for a Certificate of Appropriateness within not more than forty-five (45) days after the filing thereof by the owner or occupant of an historic property, or of a structure, site, or work of art located within an historic district. Evidence of approval shall be by a Certificate of Appropriateness issued by the Commission.

(2) Failure of the Commission to act within said forty-five (45) days shall constitute approval, and no other evidence of approval shall be needed.

J. *Necessary Actions to be Taken by Commission upon Rejection of Application for Certificate of Appropriateness.*

(1) In the event the Commission rejects an application, it shall state its reasons for doing so, and shall transmit a record of such actions and reasons, in writing, to the applicant. The Commission may suggest alternative courses of action it thinks proper if it disapproves of the application submitted. The applicant, if he or she so desires, may make modifications to the plans and may resubmit the application at any time after doing so.

(2) In cases where the application covers a material change in the appearance of a structure which would require the issuance of a building permit, the rejection of the application for a Certificate of Appropriateness by the Commission shall be binding upon the building inspector or other administrative officer charged with issuing building permits and, in such a case, no building permit shall be issued.

K. *Undue Hardship.*

Where, by reason of unusual circumstances, the strict application of any provision of this Ordinance would result in the exceptional practical difficulty or undue hardship upon any owner of a specific property, the Commission, in passing upon applications, shall have the power to vary or modify strict adherence to said provisions, or to interpret the meaning of said provisions, so as to relieve such difficulty or hardship; provided such variances, modifications, or interpretations shall remain in harmony with the general purpose and intent of said provisions, so that the architectural or historical integrity, or character of the property, shall be conserved and substantial justice done. In granting variances, the Commission may impose such reasonable and additional stipulations and conditions as will, in its judgment, best fulfill the purpose of this Ordinance. An undue hardship shall be a situation not of the person's own making, which is: a) a problem unique to a specific property, or b) in order to comply with this Ordinance, the person will conflict with another Ordinance of the (City/County).

L. *Requirement of Conformance with Certificate of Appropriateness.*

Work not in accordance with an issued Certificate of Appropriateness shall be halted before it is completed.

M. *Certificate of Appropriateness Void if Construction not Commenced.*

A Certificate of Appropriateness shall become void unless construction is commenced within six (6) months of date of issuance. Certificates of Appropriateness shall be issued for a period of eighteen (18) months and are renewable.

N. *Recording of Applications for Certificate of Appropriateness.*

The Commission shall keep a public record of all applications for Certificates of Appropriateness, and of all the Commission's proceedings in connection with said application.

O. *Acquisition of Property.*

The Commission may, where such action is authorized by the local governing body, and is reasonably necessary or appropriate for the preservation of a unique historic property, enter into negotiations with the owner for the acquisition by gift, purchase, exchange, or otherwise, of the property or any interest therein.

P. *Appeals.*

Any person adversely affected by any determination made by the Commission relative to the issuance or denial of a Certificate of Appropriateness may appeal such determination to the (City Council/County Commission); the appeal must be applied for within fifteen (15) days after notification is sent. The (City/County) may approve, modify, or reject the determination made by the Commission, if the governing body finds that the Commission abused its discretion in reaching its decision. Appeals from decisions of the (City/County) made pursuant to the Georgia Historic Preservation Act may be taken to the Superior Court of the County, in the manner provided by law, for appeals from conviction for municipal or county ordinance violations.

Section V

Demolition or Relocation Applications

A. *Authority to Comment on Demolition Permit Applications.*

The Commission shall have the authority to comment on any request for a permit to demolish or relocate a structure within an historic district, or classified as an historic landmark.

B. *Actions Acceptable in Reaction to Application for Demolition or Relocation Permit.*

The Commission shall have the authority to delay, or merely comment upon, demolition or relocation permits within its jurisdiction.

OPTION:

The Commission shall have the authority to deny demolition or relocation permits within its jurisdiction.

C. *Consideration of Pre-Demolition Plans.*

A Public Hearing shall be scheduled for each application for demolition. This hearing shall be scheduled prior to the delay period specified.

D. *Considerations of Post-Demolition Plans.*

The Commission shall not grant demolition permission without reviewing at the same time the plans for the building that would replace the structure.

E. *Demolition or Relocation Criteria.*

(1) Whenever a property owner shows that a building classified as

Historic is incapable of earning an economic return on its value, as appraised by a qualified real estate appraiser, and the Commission fails to approve the issuance of a Certificate of Appropriateness, such building may be demolished; provided, however, that before a demolition permit is issued, notice of proposed demolition shall be given as follows:

a) for buildings rated Historic—Six (6) months
b) for buildings rated Non-Historic—Two (2) months
c) for buildings rated Intrusion—No delay

(2) Notice shall be posted on the premises of the building or structure proposed for demolition in a location clearly visible from the street. In addition, notice shall be published in a newspaper of general local circulation at least three times prior to the date of the permit, and the first notice of which shall be published no more than fifteen (15) days after the application for a permit to demolish is filed. The purpose of this section is to further the purposes of this Ordinance by preserving historic buildings which are important to the education, culture, traditions, and the economic values of the (City/County) and to give the (City's/County's) interested persons, historical societies, or organizations the opportunity to acquire or to arrange for the preservation of such buildings. The Commission may at any time during such stay approve a Certificate of Appropriateness, in which event a permit shall be issued without further delay.

OPTION:

Upon receipt of an application for a Certificate of Appropriateness for demolition or relocation, the Commission shall make a determination, supported by a written report, whether one or more of the following criteria are met:

(1) The structure is of such interest or quality that it would reasonably meet national, state, or local criteria for designation as an historic or architectural landmark.

(2) The structure is of such unusual or uncommon design texture or materials that it could not be reproduced or be reproduced only with great difficulty and expense.

(3) Retention of the structure would aid substantially in preserving and protecting a structure which meets criterion (1) or (2) hereinabove.

Where the Commission determines that one or more of these criteria are met, no Certificate of Appropriateness shall be issued and the application shall be denied.

Section VI

Maintenance of Historic Property

A. *Ordinary Repair.*

Ordinary maintenance or repair of any exterior architectural feature in or on an historic property, that does not involve a material change in design, material, or outer appearance thereof, is excluded from review.

B. *Conformity to Existing Building Codes.*

Nothing in this Ordinance shall be construed as to exempt property owners from complying with existing City or County building codes, nor to prevent any property owner from making any use of his property not prohibited by other statutes, ordinances, or regulations.

Section VII

Penalty Provisions

Violations of any provisions of this Ordinance shall be punished in the same manner as provided by charter or local law for punishment of violations of other validly-enacted ordinances of the (City/County).

Section VIII

Severability

In the event that any section, subsection, sentence, clause, or phrase of this Ordinance shall be declared or adjudged invalid or unconstitutional, such adjudication shall in no manner affect the other sections, sentences, clauses, or phrases of this Ordinance, which shall remain in full force and effect, as if the section, subsection, sentence, clause, or phrase so declared or adjudged invalid or unconstitutional were not originally a part thereof.

Section IX

Repealer

All ordinances and parts of ordinances in conflict with this Ordinance are hereby repealed.

Section X

Effective Date

This Ordinance shall become effective upon its approval by the (jurisdiction).

Section XI

Definitions

(a) *"Certificate of Appropriateness"* —Means a document evidencing approval by the Historic Preservation Commission of an application to make a material change in the appearance of a designated historic property or of a property located within a designated historic district.

(b) *"Exterior Architectural Features"* —Means the architectural style, general design, and general arrangment of the exterior of a building or other structure, including but not limited to the kind or texture of the building material and the type and style of all windows, doors, signs and other appurtenant architectural fixtures, features, details or elements relative to the foregoing.

(c) *"Exterior Environmental Features"* —Means all those aspects of the landscape or the development of the site which affect the historical character of the property.

(d) *"Historic District"* —Means a geographically definable area which contains structures, sites, works of art or a combination thereof which exhibit a special historical, architectural, or environmental character as designated by (Mayor and Council/County Commissioners).

(e) *"Historic Property"* —Means an individual structure, site, or work of art which exhibits a special historical, architectural, or environmental character as designated by (Mayor and Council/County Commissioners).

(f) *"Material Change in Appearance"* —Means a change that will affect either the exterior architectural or environmental features of an historic property or any structure, site or work of art within an historic district, and may include any one or more of the following:

(1) A reconstruction or alteration of the size, shape, or facade of an historic property, including any of its architectural elements or details;
(2) Demolition of an historic structure;
(3) Commencement of excavation for construction purposes;
(4) A change in the location of advertising visible from the public right-of-way;
(5) The erection, alteration, restoration or removal of any building or other structure within an historic property or district, including walls, fences, steps and pavements, or other appurtenant features.

THEREFORE BE IT RESOLVED, that the (jurisdiction) does hereby ordain, resolve, and enact the foregoing Historic Preservation Commission Ordinance for the (jurisdiction).

Adopted this _____ day of _____ , 19 _____ .

Date of Implementation: _____ day of _____ , 19 _____ .

APPROVED:

_____

Mayor or Chairman,
County Commissioners

ATTEST:

_____

Clerk

Appendix B

Rules of Procedure—A Model
(CITY/COUNTY) HISTORIC
PRESERVATION COMMISSION
Adopted _____ , 19 _____ .

I. PURPOSE

To establish procedures for processing applications for certificates of appropriateness for (1) any changes in the external appearance of existing structures; (2) design of new structures; and (3) demolition of landmarks and existing structures within designated historic districts.

II. GENERAL RULES

The (City/County) Historic Preservation Committee shall be governed by the terms of the (City/County) Historic Preservation Ordinance as contained in the Code of Ordinances for the (City/County) and by the terms of Georgia Code 44-10-20 through 44-10-31 as they may be amended or revised.

III. JURISDICTION

The jurisdiction for requiring certificates of appropriateness as required by the (City/County) Historic Preservation Ordinance shall be delineated on the official zoning map on file in the Planning Department (or, where zoning is not in force, on an official map).

IV. MEMBERS, OFFICERS, AND DUTIES

A. *General.* The Commission shall be composed of _____ members, the majority of whom shall have demonstrated special interest, experience, or education in history, architecture and other design-related professions.

B. *Chairman.* A chairman shall be elected by the voting members of the Historic Preservation Commission. His/her term shall be for one year, and he/she may serve for no more than two consecutive terms. The chairman shall decide all points of order and procedure, subject to these rules, unless directed otherwise by a majority of the Commission in session at the time. The chairman shall appoint any committees found necessary to investigate any matters before the Commission.

C. *Vice-Chairman.* A vice-chairman shall be elected by the Commission from among its members in the same manner as the chairman and shall be eligible for re-election. He/she shall serve as acting chairman in the absence of the chairman, and at such times he/she shall have the same powers and duties as the chairman.

D. *Secretary.* A member of the planning staff, building department, or another employee designated by the (Mayor/Chairman), shall serve as secretary to the Commission. The secretary, subject to the direction of the chairman of the Commission, shall keep all records, shall conduct all correspondence of the Commission, and shall generally supervise the clerical work of the Commission. The secretary shall not be eligible to vote upon any matter.

E. *Elections.* Terms for officers shall begin in _____ . Members shall be notified in writing of the election of officers at least thirty (30) days prior to the regular _____ meeting.

F. *Terms of Appointments.* Terms of appointment for Commission members shall be three years from date of appointment, ending December 31, except in the initial organization of the Commission.

G. *Attendance at Meetings.* Should a member fail to attend three consecutive regular meetings of the Board, and should there be no adequate excuse for such absences, the chairman, with the concurrence of a majority of the entire Board, shall recommend to the appropriate authority that a vacancy be declared and that the vacated position be filled.

H. *Applications Involving Members.* No Commission member shall take part in the hearing, consideration or determination of any case in which he/she is personally or financially interested.

V. MEETINGS

A. Regular meetings of the Commission shall be held on (day of week) or each month at (time) in the (designated building); provided that meetings may be held at some other convenient place if directed by the chairman in advance of the meeting.

B. *Special Meetings.* Special meetings of the Commission may be called at any time by the chairman. At least twenty-four (24) hours' notice of the time and place of special meetings shall be given, by the secretary or by the chairman, to each member of the Commission; provided that this requirement may be waived by action of a majority of all the members.

C. *Cancellation of Meetings.* Whenever there is no business for the Commission, the chairman may dispense with a regular meeting by giving notice to all the members not less than twenty-four (24) hours prior to the time set for the meeting.

D. *Quorum.* A quorum shall consist of (a majority designated by number) of members of the Commission.

E. *Conduct of Meetings.* All meetings shall be open to the public.

The order of business at regular meetings shall be as follows: (a) roll call; (b) reading of minutes of previous meetings; (c) report of committees; (d) unfinished business; (e) new business.

F. *Review Criteria.* In reviewing applications for certificates of appropriateness, the Commission shall take into account the historic and architectural significance of the structure and shall maintain maps showing the historic and architectural significance of structures. In its review the Commission shall also take into account the following elements to ensure that the exterior form and appearance of the structure is consistent with the historical or visual character of the District:

1. The height of the building in relation to the average height of the nearest adjacent and opposite buildings.
2. The setback and placement on lot of the building in relation to the average setback and placement of the nearest adjacent and opposite buildings.
3. Exterior construction materials, including textures and patterns but not to include color.
4. Architectural detailing, such as lintels, cornices, brick bond, and foundation materials.
5. Roof shapes, forms, and materials.
6. Proportions, shapes, positionings and locations, patterns and sizes of any elements of fenestration.
7. General form and proportions of buildings and structures.
8. Appurtenant fixtures and other features such as lighting.
9. Structural condition and soundness.

The Commission may designate more explicit design criteria as it deems necessary. (Note: It is within this section that local design guidelines should be noted.)

G. *Consideration of Applications.* Any party may appear in person or by agent or attorney at the meeting. The order of business for consideration of applications for certificates of appropriateness shall be as follows:

(a) The chairman, or such person as he or she shall direct, shall give a preliminary statement concerning the application;
(b) The applicant shall present the arguments in support of his or her application;
(c) Persons opposed to granting the application shall present the arguments against the application;
(d) Statements of arguments submitted by any official, commission, or department of the (Jurisdiction), any state agency, or any local historical, preservation or neighborhood association shall be presented as directed by the chairman;
(e) The chairman, or such person as he or she shall direct, shall summarize the evidence which has been presented,

giving all parties an opportunity to make objections or corrections; and

(f) The Commission shall thereafter proceed to deliberate whether to grant the application or to deny it.

(g) Testimony shall be sworn unless all parties agree to waive the oath.

(h) Procedures may be modified by concurrence of all parties and the Commission itself.

The Commission may, in its discretion, view the premises and obtain additional facts concerning any application before arriving at a decision. All decisions of the Commission shall be supported by appropriate findings of fact, and, where necessary to effectuate the purposes of the ordinance, shall be accompanied by such conditions and/or recommendations as it may determine to be reasonable under the circumstances.

In considering applications, witnesses may be called and factual evidence may be submitted, but the board shall not be limited to consideration of such evidence as would be admissible in a court of law.

H. *Vote.* The vote of a majority of those members present shall be sufficient to decide matters before the Commission, provided a quorum is present. No Commission member shall participate in the decision of any matter in which he or she has a personal or financial interest.

VI. APPLICATION PROCEDURES

A. An application must be filed in the Planning Department at least ten (10) working days prior to the next meeting of the Commission, accompanied by sketches, drawings, photographs, specifications, descriptions, etc., of the proposed project.

B. Using stamped, self-addressed envelopes supplied by the applicant, the Planning Department shall notify by mail, not less than one week prior to the meeting at which the matter is to be heard, the affected property owners within:

1. 100 feet on all sides of the subject property for applications which involve a material change in the property; or

2. 500 feet on all sides of the subject property for applications which involve a demolition or relocation.

C. The applicant and affected property owners shall be given an opportunity to be heard at the meeting at which the application is presented.

D. In cases where the Commission deems it necessary, it may hold a public hearing concerning the application.

E. The Commission must issue or deny a certificate of appropriateness within forty-five (45) days after the filing of the application, except when the time limit has been extended by mutual agreement between the applicant and the Commission.

F. If the application is approved, the secretary for the Commission shall transmit a certificate of appropriateness in letter form, clearly describing the nature of the work which has been approved. The secretary shall attach a copy of the minutes of the meeting at which approval was granted and placard form of a certificate of appropriateness to be displayed on the project. A copy of this information shall be forwarded to the Inspections Department which is responsible for its enforcement.

G. If an application is denied, a copy of the minutes of the meeting and written reasons for denial shall be made available to the applicant.

VII. AMENDMENTS

These rules may, within the limits allowed by law, be amended at any time by an affirmative vote of not less than three-fourths (¾) of the members of the Commission, provided that such amendment shall have first been presented to the membership in writing at a regular or special meeting preceding the meeting at which the vote is taken.

Adapted from Rules of Procedure, as adopted by the Chapel Hill Historic District Commission, Chapel Hill, North Carolina.

CHAIRMAN'S CHECKLIST FOR PREPARING AND CONDUCTING A MEETING

Before the Meeting

1. Check with staff to insure that:
   a. Notices have been sent out.
   b. All applications have been properly advertised/mailed.
   c. All applications have been completed and mailed to members in advance.
   d. Availability of minutes has been checked.
   e. Meeting room is available and in order:
      (1) Name placards in place
      (2) Adequate seating for petitioners, etc.
      (3) Maps up/photographs or slides ready
      (4) Bible for oaths
      (5) Tape recorder.
   f. Check on quorum, absences, etc.
2. Visit each property on agenda on day of meeting.

At the Meeting

1. Call roll (note excused absences); record presence of quorum.

2. Ask for corrections or additions to minutes; adopt same.
3. Call for committee reports (when appropriate).
4. Conduct unfinished business.
5. Conduct new business.
6. Follow this procedure in hearing of cases:
   a. Call case according to agenda/Check for conflicts of interest/ Record.
   b. If opposition or controversy, swear witness, including attorneys.
   c. Call secretary to present facts of application:
      (1) Identify property on map
      (2) Indicate level of significance
      (3) Indicate impacts on adjoining property and visibility or proposed work from the street.
   d. Call upon applicant or representative for any additional information or corrections.
   e. Ask for opponents/Record by name and address.
   f. Ask secretary if any planning staff or other public representatives have any comments to be submitted for the record.
   g. Ask for presentations from any state agency or local group.
   h. Summarize evidence and facts if pro and con arguments are made; if not, note for record that absent objections, presentations appearing in record are uncontested.
   i. Proceed to discussion with respect to "congruity" vis a vis:
      (1) Height
      (2) Setback and placement
      (3) Materials (textures and patterns but no color)
      (4) Architectural detailing
      (5) Roof shapes, forms, materials
      (6) Fenestration proportions, shapes, positions and location, pattern
      (7) General form and proportions of buildings and structures
      (8) Appurtenant features and fixtures: lighting, walls, fences, landscaping
      (9) Structural condition and soundness.
   j. Accept motion for findings of fact that proposal is/is not incongruous with historic aspects of the district with respect to each item above "for the reason that . . ." Second. Discuss. Adopt.
   k. Discuss appropriateness of imposing conditions (specific wording).
   l. Call for motion that application for Certificate of Appropriateness be: accepted/rejected/approved subject to conditions/case to be continued for further information/Second/Discuss/Vote.

(Call on each commission member for comments following motion made and seconded in (j) above.)

   m. Thank applicant/neighbors/associations for coming. Invite to stay, but indicate they may leave and will receive formal notification from Inspections Division.

n. Proceed to next application.

Reproduced with permission of Chapel Hill Historic District Commission, Chapel Hill, N.C.

Appendix C

The Secretary of the Interior's Standards for Rehabilitation and Guidelines for Rehabilitating Historic Buildings

"Rehabilitation means the process of returning a property to a state of utility, through repair or alteration, which makes possible an efficient contemporary use while preserving those portions and features of property which are significant to its historic, architectural, and cultural values."

The following "Standards for Rehabilitation" shall be used by the Secretary of the Interior when determining if a rehabilitation project qualifies as a "certified rehabilitation" pursuant to the Tax Reform Act of 1976, the Revenue Act of 1978, and the Economic Recovery Tax Act of 1981. These standards are a section of the Secretary's "Standards for Historic Preservation Projects" and appear in Title 36 of the Code of Federal Regulations, Part 67 (formerly 36 CFR Part 1208).

1. Every reasonable effort shall be made to provide a compatible use for a property which requires minimal alteration of the buildings, structure, or site and its environment, or to use a property for its originally intended purpose.
2. The distinguishing original qualities or character of a building, structure, or site and its environment shall not be destroyed. The removal or alteration of any historic material or distinctive architectural features should be avoided when possible.
3. All buildings, structures, and sites shall be recognized as products of their own time. Alterations that have no historical basis and which seek to create an earlier appearance shall be discouraged.
4. Changes which may have taken place in the course of time are evidence of the history and development of a building, structure, or site and its environment. These changes may have acquired significance in their own right, and this significance shall be recognized and respected.
5. Distinctive stylistic features or examples of skilled craftsmanship which characterize a building, structure, or site shall be treated with sensitivity.
6. Deteriorated architectural features shall be repaired rather than replaced, wherever possible. In the event replacement is necessary, the new material should match the material being replaced in composition, design, color, texture, and other visual qualities. Repair or replacement of missing architectural features should be based on accurate duplications of features, substantiated by historic, physical, or pictorial evidence rather than on conjectural designs or the availability of different architectural elements from other buildings or structures.

7. The surface cleaning of structures shall be undertaken with the gentlest means possible. Sandblasting and other cleaning methods that will damage the historic building materials shall not be undertaken.
8. Every reasonable effort shall be made to protect and preserve archeological resources affected by, or adjacent to, any project.
9. Contemporary design for alterations and additions to existing properties shall not be discouraged when such alterations and additions do not destroy significant historical, architectural or cultural material, and such design is compatible with the size, scale, color, material, and character of the property, neighborhood or environment.
10. Wherever possible, new additions or alterations to structures shall be done in such a manner that if such additions or alterations were to be removed in the future, the essential form and integrity of the structure would be unimpaired.

Guidelines for Applying
the Secretary of the Interior's
Standards for Rehabilitation

The following guidelines are designed to help individual property owners formulate plans for the rehabilitation, preservation, and continued use of historic buildings consistent with the intent of the Secretary of the Interior's "Standards for Rehabilitation." The guidelines pertain to buildings of all occupancy and construction types, sizes, and materials. They apply to permanent and temporary construction on the exterior and interior of historic buildings as well as new attached or adjacent construction.

Techniques, treatments, and methods consistent with the Secretary's "Standards for Rehabilitation" are listed in the "recommended" column on the left. Not all recommendations listed under a treatment will apply to each project proposal. Rehabilitation approaches, materials, and methods which may adversely affect a building's architectural and historic qualities are listed in the "not recommended" column. Every effort will be made to update and expand the guidelines as additional techniques and treatments become known.

Specific information on rehabilitation and preservation technology may be obtained by writing to the Technical Preservation Services Division, National Park Service, U.S. Department of the Interior, Washington, D.C. 20240, or the appropriate State Historic Preservation Officer. Advice should also be sought from qualified professionals, including architects, architectural historians, and archeologists skilled in the preservation, restoration, and rehabilitation of old buildings.

THE ENVIRONMENT

Recommended

Retaining distinctive features such as the size, scale, mass, color, and materials of buildings, including roofs, porches, and stairways that give a neighborhood its distinguishing character.

Retaining landscape features such as parks, gardens, street lights, signs, benches, walkways, streets, alleys, and building setbacks that have traditionally linked buildings to their environment.

Using new plant materials, fencing, walkways, street lights, signs, and benches that are compatible with the character of the neighborhood in size, scale, material, and color.

Not Recommended

Introducing new construction into neighborhoods that is incompatible with the character of the district because of size, scale, color, and materials.

Destroying the relationship of buildings and their environment by widening existing streets, changing paving material, or by introducing inappropriately located new streets and parking lots that are incompatible with the character of the neighborhood.

Introducing signs, street lighting, benches, new plant materials, fencing, walkways and paving materials that are out of scale or are inappropriate to the neighborhood.

BUILDING SITE

Recommended

Identifying plants, trees, fencing, walkways, outbuildings, and other elements that might be an important part of the property's history and development.

Retaining plants, trees, fencing, walkways, street lights, signs, and benches that reflect the property's history and development.

Basing decisions for new site work on actual knowledge of the past appearance of the property found in photographs, drawings, newspapers, and tax records. If changes are made they should be carefully evaluated in light of the past appearance of the site.

Providing proper site and roof drainage to assure that water does not splash against building or foundation walls, nor drain toward the building.

Not Recommended

Making changes to the appearance of the site by removing old plants, trees, fencing, walkways, outbuildings, and other elements before evaluating their importance in the property's history and development.

Leaving plant materials and trees in close proximity to the buildings that may be causing deterioration of the historic fabric.

Archeological features

Recommended	Not Recommended
Leaving known archeological resources intact.	Installing underground utilities, pavements, and other modern features that disturb archeological resources.
Minimizing disturbance of terrain around the structure, thus reducing the possibility of destroying unknown archeological resources.	Introducing heavy machinery or equipment into areas where their presence may disturb archeological resources.
Arranging for an archeological survey of all terrain that must be disturbed during the rehabilitation program. The survey should be conducted by a professional archeologist.	

BUILDING: STRUCTURAL SYSTEMS

Recommended	Not Recommended
Recognizing the special problems inherent in the structural systems of historic buildings, especially where there are visible signs of cracking, deflection, or failure.	Disturbing existing foundations with new excavations that undermine the structural stability of the building.
Undertaking stabilization and repair of weakened structural members and systems.	Leaving known structural problems untreated that will cause continuing deterioration and will shorten the life of the structure.
Replacing historically important structural members only when necessary. Supplementing existing structural systems when damaged or inadequate.	

BUILDING: EXTERIOR FEATURES

Masonry: Adobe, brick, stone, terra cotta, concrete, stucco and mortar

Recommended*	Not Recommended
Retaining original masonry and mortar, whenever possible, without the application of any surface treatment.	Applying waterproof or water repellent coatings or surface consolidation treatments unless required to solve a specific technical problem that has been studied

---

*For more information consult Preservation Briefs: 1: "The Cleaning and Waterproof Coating of Masonry Buildings" and Preservation Briefs: 2: "Repointing Mortar Joints in Historic Brick Buildings" (Washington, D.C.: Heritage Conservation and Recreation Service, 1975 and 1976). Both are available from the Government Printing Office or State Historic Preservation Officers.

(Masonry, cont.)

Recommended	Not Recommended

Repointing only those mortar joints where there is evidence of moisture problems or when sufficient mortar is missing to allow water to stand in the mortar joint.

and identified. Coatings are frequently unnecessary, expensive, and can accelerate deterioration of the masonry.

Repointing mortar joints that do not need repointing. Using electric saws and hammers to remove mortar can seriously damage adjacent brick.

Duplicating old mortar in composition, color, and texture.

Duplicating old mortar in joint size, method of application, and joint profile.

Repairing stucco with a stucco mixture that duplicates the original as closely as possible in appearance and texture.

Repointing with mortar of high Portland cement content can often create a bond that is stronger than the building material. This can cause deterioration as a result of the differing coefficient of expansion and the differing porosity of the material and the mortar.

Cleaning masonry only when necessary to halt deterioration or to remove graffiti and stains and always with the gentlest method possible, such as low pressure water and soft natural bristle brushes.

Repointing with mortar joints of a differing size or joint profile, texture, or color.

Repairing or replacing, where necessary, deteriorated material with new material that duplicates the old as closely as possible.

Replacing missing significant architectural features, such as cornices, brackets, railings, and shutters.

Retaining the original or early color and texture of masonry surfaces, including early signage wherever possible. Brick or stone surfaces may have been painted or whitewashed for practical and aesthetic reasons.

Sandblasting, including dry and wet grit and other abrasives, brick or stone surfaces; this method of cleaning erodes the surface of the material and accelerates deterioration. Using chemical cleaning products that would have an adverse chemical reaction with the masonry materials, i.e., acid on limestone or marble.

Applying new material which is inappropriate or was unavailable when the building was constructed, such as artificial brick siding, artificial cast stone, or brick veneer.

Removing architectural features such as cornices, brackets, railings, shutters, window architraves, and doorway pediments.

Removing paint from masonry surfaces indiscriminately. This may subject the building to damage and change its appearance.

Wood: Clapboard, weatherboard, shingles and other wooden siding

Recommended	Not Recommended
Retaining and preserving significant architectural features, wherever possible. Repairing or replacing, where necessary, deteriorated material that duplicates in size, shape, and texture the old as closely as possible.	Removing architectural features such as siding, cornices, brackets, window architraves, and doorway pediments. These are, in most cases, an essential part of a building's character and appearance that illustrate the continuity of growth and change. Resurfacing frame buildings with new material that is inappropriate or was unavailable when the building was constructed such as artificial stone, brick veneer, asbestos or asphalt shingles, and plastic or aluminum siding. Such material can also contribute to the deterioration of the structure from moisture and insects.

Architectural Metals: Cast iron, steel, pressed tin, aluminum and zinc

Recommended	Not Recommended
Retaining original material, whenever possible. Cleaning when necessary with the appropriate method. Metals should be cleaned by methods that do not abrade the surface.	Removing architectural features that are an essential part of a building's character and appearance, illustrating the continuity of growth and change. Exposing metals which were intended to be protected from the environment. Do not use cleaning methods which alter the color, texture, and tone of the metal.

Roofs and Roofing

Recommended	Not Recommended
Preserving the original roof shape. Retaining the original roofing material, whenever possible. Providing adequate roof drainage and insuring that the roofing materials provide a weather tight covering for the structure. Replacing deteriorated roof coverings with new material that matches the old in composition, size, shape, color, and texture. Preserving or replacing, where necessary, all architectural features that give the roof its essential character, such as dormer windows, cupolas, cornices,	Changing the essential character of the roof by adding inappropriate features such as dormer windows, vents, or skylights. Applying new roofing material that is inappropriate to the style and period of the building and neighborhood. Replacing deteriorated roof coverings with new materials that differ to such an extent from the old in composition, size, shape, color, and texture that the appearance of the building is altered. Stripping the roof of architectural features important to its character.

brackets, chimneys, cresting, and weather vanes.

Windows and Doors

Recommended*

Retaining and repairing window and door openings, frames, sash, glass, doors, lintels, sills, pediments, architraves, hardware, awnings, and shutters where they contribute to the architectural and historic character of the building.

Improving the thermal performance of existing windows and doors through aiding or replacing weatherstripping and adding storm windows and doors which are compatible with the character of the building and which do not damage window or door frames.

Not Recommended

Introducing or changing the location or size of windows, doors, and other openings that alter the architectural and historic character of the building.

Replacing window and door features on significant facades with historically and architecturally incompatible materials such as anodized aluminum, mirrored or tinted glass.

Removing window and door features that can be repaired where such features contribute to the historic and architectural character of the building.

Changing the size or arrangement of window panes, muntins, and rails where they contribute to the architectural and historic character of the building.

Installing on significant facades shutters, screens, blinds, security grills, and awnings which are historically inappropriate and which detract from the character of the building.

Installing new exterior storm windows and doors which are inappropriate in size or color, which are inoperable, or which require removal of original windows and doors.

Installing interior storm windows that allow moisture to accumulate and damage the window.

Replacing sashes which contribute to the character of a building with those that are incompatible in size, configuration, and reflective qualities or which alter the setback relationship between window and wall.

---

*For more information consult Preservation Briefs: 3: "Conserving Energy in Historic Buildings" (Washington, D.C.: Heritage Conservation and Recreation Service, 1978). It is available from the Government Printing Office or State Historic Preservation Officers.

Replacing missing or irreparable windows on significant facades with new windows that match the original in material, size, general muntin and mullion proportion and configuration, and reflective qualities of the glass.

Installing heating/air conditioning units in the window frames when the sash and frames may be damaged. Window installations should be considered only when all other viable heating/cooling systems would result in significant damage to historic materials.

Storefronts

Recommended

Retaining and repairing existing storefronts including windows, sashes, doors, transoms, signage, and decorative features where such features contribute to the architectural and historic character of the building.

Where original or early storefronts no longer exist or are too deteriorated to save, retaining the commercial character of the building through 1) contemporary design which is compatible with the scale, design, materials, color, and texture of the historic buildings; or 2) an accurate restoration of the storefront based on historical research and physical evidence.

Not Recommended

Introducing a storefront or new design element on the ground floor, such as an arcade, which alters the architectural and historic character of the building and its relationship with the street or its setting or which causes destruction of significant historic fabric.

Using materials which detract from the historic or architectural character of the building, such as mirrored glass.

Altering the entrance through a significant storefront.

Entrances, porches, and steps

Recommended

Retaining porches and steps that are appropriate to the building and its development. Porches or additions reflecting later architectural styles are often important to the building's historical integrity and, wherever possible, should be retained.

Repairing or replacing, where necessary, deteriorated architectural features of wood, iron, cast iron, terra cotta, tile, and brick.

Not Recommended

Removing or altering porches and steps that are appropriate to the building's development and style.

Stripping porches and steps of original material and architectural features, such as hand rails, balusters, columns, brackets, and roof decorations of wood, iron, cast iron, terra cotta, tile and brick.

Enclosing porches and steps in a manner that destroys their intended appearance.

Exterior Finishes

Recommended	Not Recommended
Discovering the historic paint colors and finishes of the structure and repainting with those colors to illustrate the distinctive character of the property.	Removing paint and finishes down to the bare surface; strong paint strippers, whether chemical or mechanical, can permanently damage the surface. Also, stripping obliterates evidence of the historical paint finishes.
	Repainting with colors that cannot be documented through research and investigation to be appropriate to the building and neighborhood.

BUILDING: INTERIOR FEATURES

Recommended	Not Recommended
Retaining original material, architectural features, and hardware, whenever possible, such as stairs, elevators, hand rails, balusters, ornamental columns, cornices, baseboards, doors, doorways, windows, mantel pieces, paneling, lighting fixtures, parquet or mosaic flooring.	Removing original material, architectural features, and hardware, except where essential for safety or efficiency.
Repairing or replacing, where necessary, deteriorated material with new material that duplicates the old as closely as possible.	Replacing interior doors and transoms without investigating alternative fire protection measures or possible code variances.
Retaining original plaster, whenever possible.	Installing new decorative material and paneling which destroys significant architectural features or was unavailable when the building was constructed, such as vinyl plastic or imitation wood wall and floor coverings, except in utility areas such as bathrooms and kitchens.
Discovering and retaining original paint colors, wallpapers, and other decorative motifs or, where necessary, replacing them with colors, wallpapers, or decorative motifs based on the original.	Removing plaster to expose brick to give the wall an appearance it never had.
Where required by code, enclosing an important interior stairway in such a way as to retain its character. In many cases, glazed fire rated walls may be used.	Changing the texture and patina of exposed wooden architectural features (including structural members) and masonry surfaces through sandblasting or use of other abrasive techniques to remove paint, discoloration, and plaster, except in certain industrial or warehouse buildings where the interior masonry or plaster surfaces do not have significant design, detailing, tooling, or finish; and where wooden architectural features are not finished, molded, beaded, or worked by hand.
	Enclosing important stairways with ordinary fire rated construction which de-

(Interior Features, cont.)
Retaining the basic plan of a building, the relationship and size of rooms, corridors, and other spaces.

stroys the architectural character of the stair and the space.

Altering the basic plan of a building by demolishing principal walls, partitions, and stairways.

NEW CONSTRUCTION

Recommended

Keeping new additions and adjacent new construction to a minimum, making them compatible in scale, building materials, and texture.

Designing new work to be compatible in materials, size, color, and texture with the earlier building and the neighborhood.

Using contemporary designs compatible with the character and mood of the building or the neighborhood.

Protecting architectural details and features that contribute to the character of the building.

Placing television antennae and mechanical equipment, such as air conditioners, in an inconspicuous location.

Not Recommended

Designing new work which is incompatible with the earlier building and the neighborhood in materials, size, scale, and texture.

Imitating an earlier style or period of architecture in new additions, except in rare cases where a contemporary design would detract from the architectural unity of an ensemble or group. Especially avoid imitating an earlier style of architecture in new additions that have a completely contemporary function such as a drive-in bank or garage.

Adding new height to the building that changes the scale and character of the building. Additions in height should not be visible when viewing the principal facades.

Adding new floors or removing existing floors that destroy important architectural details, features and spaces of the building.

Placing television antennae and mechanical equipment, such as air conditioners, where they can be seen from the street.

MECHANICAL SYSTEMS: HEATING, AIR CONDITIONING, ELECTRICAL, PLUMBING, FIRE PROTECTION

Recommended

Installing necessary mechanical systems in areas and spaces that will require the least possible alteration to the structural integrity and physical appearance of the building.

Utilizing early mechanical systems, in-

Not Recommended

Causing unnecessary damage to the plan, materials, and appearance of the building when installing mechanical systems.

Attaching exterior electrical and telephone cables to the principle elevations of the building.

cluding plumbing and early lighting fixtures, where possible.

Installing the vertical runs of ducts, pipes, and cables in closets, service rooms, and wall cavities.

Insuring adequate ventilation of attics, crawl spaces, and cellars to prevent moisture problems.

Installing thermal insulation in attics and in unheated cellars and crawl spaces to conserve energy.

Installing vertical runs of ducts, pipes, and cables in places where they will be a visual intrusion.

Concealing or "making invisible" mechanical equipment in historic walls or ceiling. Frequently this concealment requires the removal of historic fabric.

Installing "dropped" acoustical ceilings to hide mechanical equipment. This destroys the proportions and character of the rooms.

Installing foam, glass fiber, or cellulose insulation into wall cavities of either wooden or masonry construction. This has been found to cause moisture problems when there is no adequate moisture barrier.

SAFETY AND CODE REQUIREMENTS

Recommended

Complying with code requirements in such a manner that the essential character of a building is preserved intact.

Working with local code officials to investigate alternative life safety measures that preserve the architectural integrity of the building.

Investigating variances for historic properties allowed under some local codes.

Installing adequate fire prevention equipment in a manner that does minimal damage to the appearance or fabric of a property.

Adding new stairways and elevators that do not alter existing exit facilities or other important architectural features and spaces of the building.

Not Recommended

Adding new stairways and elevators that alter existing exit facilities or important architectural features and spaces of the building.

National Park Service
U.S. Department of the Interior
Washington, D.C. 20240

January 1980 (rev.)

Appendix D

New Construction Design Guidelines

Factors to Be Considered
When Reviewing New Construction

A. HEIGHT: The height of the proposed building shall be visually compatible with adjacent buildings.

B. SCALE: The size of a building, the building mass of it in relation to open spaces, the windows, doors, openings, porches, and balconies shall be visually compatible with the buildings, squares, and places to which it is visually related.

C. SETBACK AND RHYTHM OF SPACING OF BUILDINGS ON STREETS: The relationship of a building to open space between it and adjoining building(s) and the road shall be visually compatible with the buildings, places, and squares to which it is visually related.

D. RELATIONSHIP OF MATERIALS, TEXTURE, DETAILS, AND COLOR: The relationship of the materials, texture, details, and color of the facade of a building shall be visually compatible with the predominant materials used in the building to which it is visually related.

E. FENESTRATION: The relationship of the width of the windows to the height of the windows in the building shall be visually compatible with buildings, squares, and places to which the building is visually related.

F. ROOF SHAPES: The shape of a building shall be visually compatible with the buildings to which it is visually related.

G. ORIENTATION OR DIRECTIONAL EXPRESSION OF FRONT ELEVATION: A building shall be visually compatible with the orientation of the buildings, squares, and places to which it is visually related, and to their directional character, whether this be vertical character, horizontal character, or non-directional character.

H. LANDSCAPING: The landscaping of an area shall attempt to maintain the historic characteristics and be visually compatible with the overall environment of the buildings, places, and squares to which it is related.

I. APPURTENANCES: Appurtenances related to a building (such as fences, stone walls, light fixtures, steps, paving, sidewalks, and signs) shall be visually compatible with the environment of the buildings, places, and squares to which they are related.

J. MODERN DESIGN: Modern designs which are sensitive to the visual characteristics of the buildings, places, and squares to which they are related shall not be discouraged.

CRITERIA

1. Height—This is a mandatory criteria that new buildings be constructed to a height within ten percent of the average height of existing adjacent buildings.

2. Proportion of buildings' front facades—The relationship between the width and height of the front elevation of the building.

WINDOW PROPORTION 2-1

3. Proportion of openings within the facade —The relationship of width to height of windows and doors.

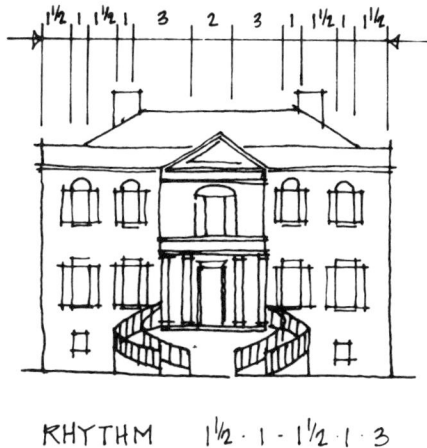

RHYTHM 1½ · 1 - 1½ · 1 · 3

4. Rhythm of solids to voids in front facade —Rhythm being an ordered recurrent alteration of strong and weak elements. Moving by an individual building, one experiences a rhythm of masses to openings.

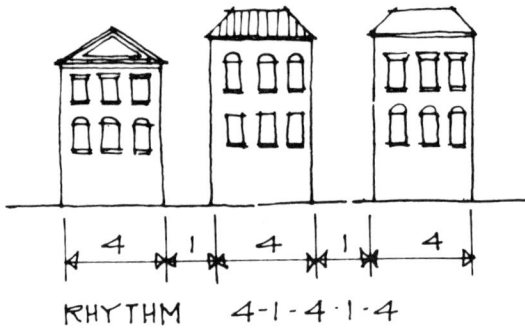

RHYTHM   4-1-4·1-4

5. Rhythm of spacing of buildings on streets—Moving past a sequence of buildings, one experiences a rhythm of recurrent building masses to spaces between them.

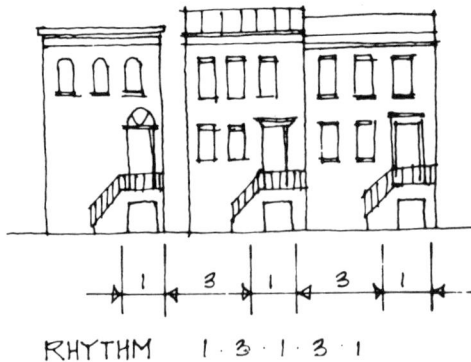

RHYTHM   1·3·1·3·1

6. Rhythm of entrance and/or porch projections—The relationship of entrances to sidewalks. Moving past a sequence of structures, one experiences a rhythm of entrances or porch projections at an intimate scale.

```
MATERIAL  /  BRICK
TEXTURE   /  RAKED JOINT
COLOR     /  RED BK., GRAY TRIM
```

7. Relationship of materials—Within an area, the predominant material may be brick, stone, stucco, wood siding or other material.

8. Relationship of textures—The predominant texture may be smooth (stucco) or rough (brick with tooled joints) or horizontal wood siding, or other textures.

9. Relationship of color—The predominant color may be that of a natural material or a painted one, or a patina colored by time. Accent or blending colors of trim is also a factor.

10. Relationship of architectural details—Details may include cornices, lintels, arches, quoins, balustrades, wrought iron work, chimneys, etc.

11. Relationship of roof shapes—The majority of buildings may have gables, wood, hip, flat roofs, or others.

WALLS & LANDSCAPING   CONTINUOUS

12. Walls of continuity—Physical ingredients such as brick walls, wrought iron fences, evergreen landscape masses, building facades, or combinations of these, form continuous cohesive walls of enclosure along the street.

13. Relationship of landscaping—There may be a predominance of a particular quality and quantity of landscaping. The concern here is more with mass and continuity.

GROUND COVERING

14. Ground cover—There may be a predominance in the use of brick pavers, cobblestones, granite blocks, tabby, or other materials.

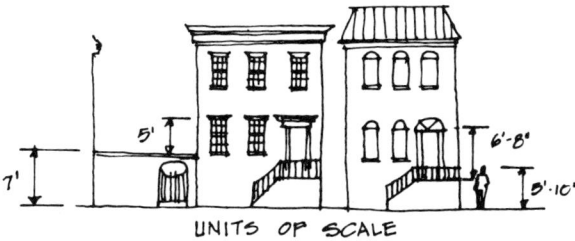

UNITS OF SCALE

15. Scale—Scale is created by the size of units of construction and architectural detail which relate to the size of man. Scale is also determined by building mass and how it relates to open space. The predominant element of scale may be brick or stone units, windows or door openings, porches or balconies, etc.

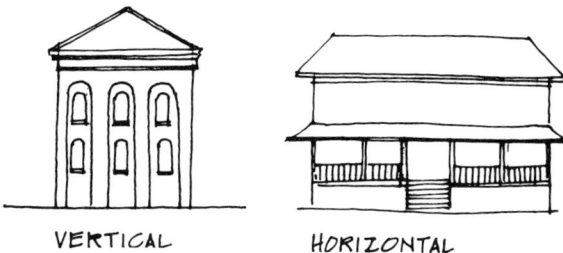

VERTICAL   HORIZONTAL

16. Directional expression of front elevation—Structural shape, placement of openings, and architectural details may give a predominantly vertical, horizontal, or a non-directional character to the building's front facade.

Mandatory Guidelines

INDIVIDUAL LOTS (INFILL)

Because infill sites relate to an established pattern and rhythm of existing buildings, both on the same and opposite sides of a street, the dominance of that pattern and rhythm must be respected.

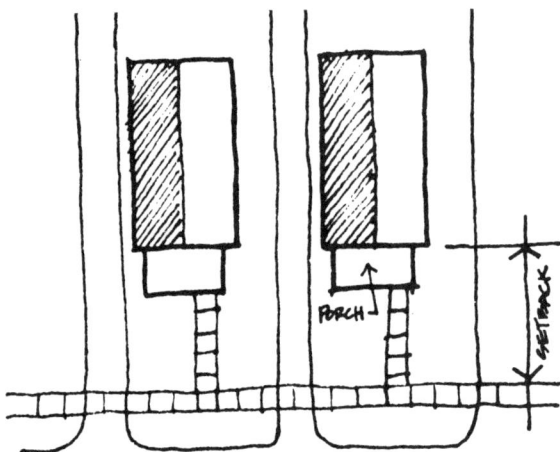

Relationship of Facades to Street—The setback from front and side yard property lines established by adjacent buildings must be maintained.

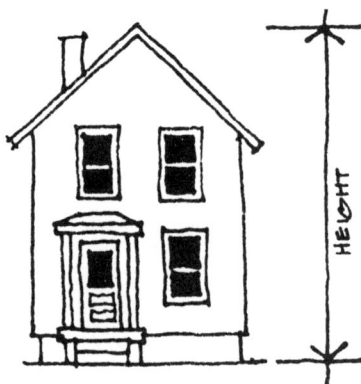

Building Height—New infill buildings must be constructed to the same number of stories and to a height which is within 10% of the average height of adjacent buildings.

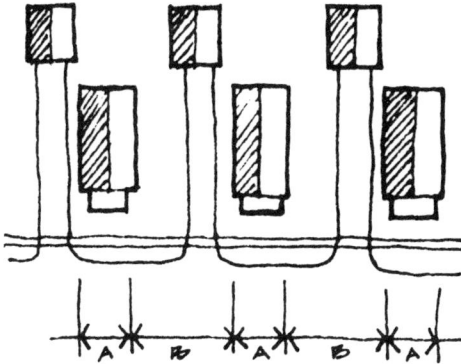

Rhythm of Facades—A rhythmic sequence along a streetscape is established by the relationship of building width to the space between building facades. Uniform lot and building width will establish a definite rhythm. Infill construction must respect the scale established by the rhythm of existing facades.

MULTIPLE LOTS (LARGER PROJECTS)

Because property made up of more than one residential size lot could allow the construction of a building which overwhelms the surrounding residential scale, mandatory guidelines should reflect this difference in development opportunity.

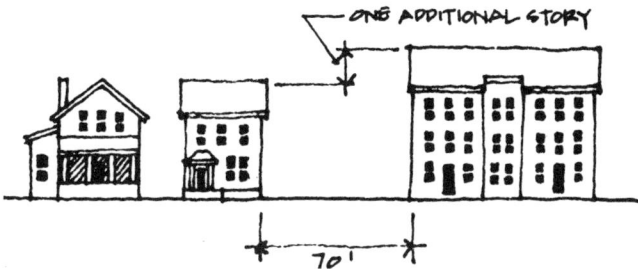

Building Height—Because larger projects are usually located further away from existing buildings than infill buildings, an additional height of no more than one story above the total height of adjacent construction is allowed over 70 feet away from any adjacent buildings.

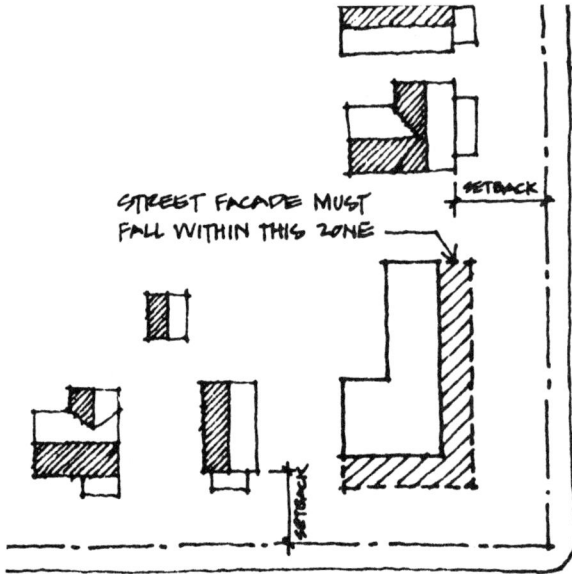

Relationship of Facade to Streets—The setback from main and side street property must be maintained within a distance which can vary within 10% of the average setback of adjacent buildings.

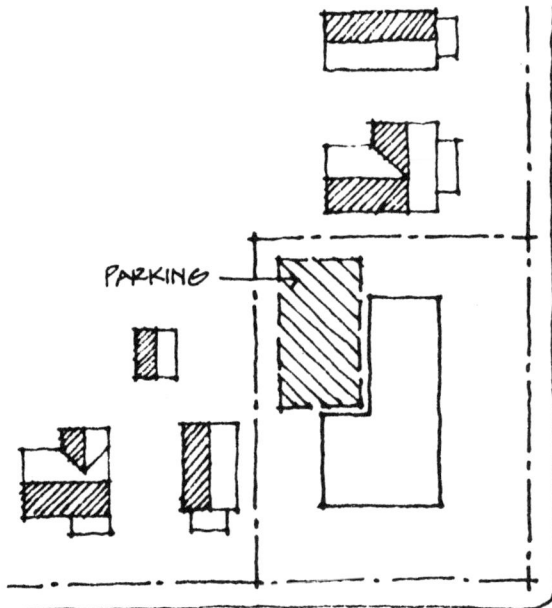

Parking—Building and parking needs must be satisfied on the same site. Adjacent sites on which existing structures are located must not be developed for additional parking.

Optional Guidelines

It should be required that a minimum of four of any of the following eight guidelines be complied with.

Roof Form—Although there is a variety of roof forms in the District, including gable, hipped, mansard and flat roofs, the roofs of new buildings should not contrast greatly with the roof type or orientation of adjacent buildings.

WINDOWS IN THE DISTRICT ARE PREDOMINANTLY VERTICAL IN PROPORTION; GREATER IN HEIGHT THAN IN WIDTH

Proportion of Openings—The relationship of the width and height of door and window openings in existing buildings should be reflected in openings of new buildings.

Rhythm of Openings—The ratio of window openings to wall surface should be respected.

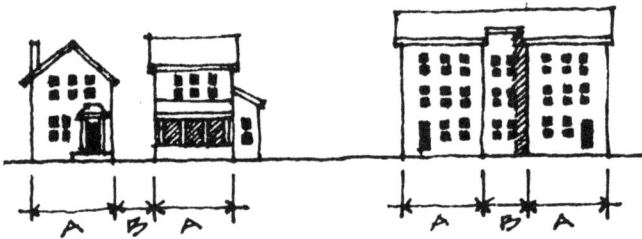

Proportion of Facades—On larger projects it should not be necessary to duplicate the scale or mass of adjacent residential buildings. However, new facades should respect facing or adjacent facades by reflecting their proportions in street-facing facades, recessing intermediate portions to reflect the width of spaces between residential structures.

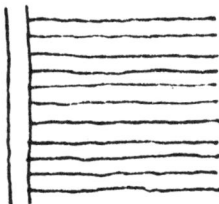
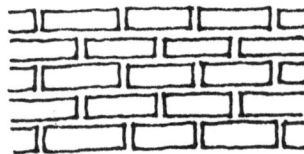

Relationship of Materials—Existing materials in the District are primarily wood and brick. Infill construction should use the same materials as those in adjacent existing buildings, or not contrast conspicuously.

Height of First Floor above Grade—The distance above street level of the first floor of adjacent existing buildings should be reflected in new construction.

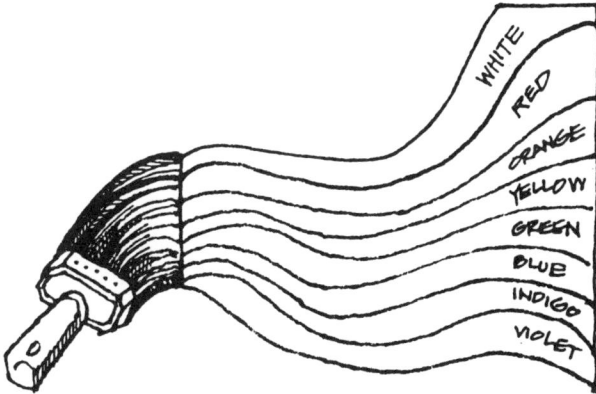

Relationship of Colors—The color of materials or painted surfaces should complement that of existing materials and appropriate historic colors.

Landscape Treatment—All aspects of site development should be in sympathy with the character of landscape development, types of plant materials, and spatial treatment of adjacent properties.

From *Historic Preservation Plan for the Central Area General Neighborhood Renewal Area, Savannah, Georgia,* with the permission of the Housing Authority of Savannah. The Savannah guidelines reflect an orientation toward rowhouses and stylistic consistency.

Appendix E*

Signage Guidelines

Signs

A development plan shall require that the appearance, size, position, method of attachment, texture of materials, color, and design of such signs is in keeping with the collective characteristics of the structures located within the appropriate Historic Zoning District. Signs as may be allowed within an Historic Zoning District shall be further limited as follows:

(a) Off-site signs shall not be permitted.

(b) Business signs shall be limited to one (1) sign only for each street frontage per premises and shall not be over five (5) feet in height.

(c) Maximum area of any sign located in an Historic Residential District shall be two (2) square feet; maximum area of any sign in an Historic Commercial District shall be sixteen (16) square feet.

(d) No sign may extend above the top of the nearest facade, eaves, or firewall of a building or structure.

(e) No sign that flashes, blinks, revolves, or is put in motion by the atmosphere shall be permitted. No visible bulbs, neon tubing, luminous paints, or plastics will be permitted as a part of any sign.

(f) Buildings and signs within the historic zone may be illuminated by remote light sources, provided that these light sources are shielded to protect adjacent properties.

(g) Real estate signs shall be removed not more than ten (10) days after the closing of a sale of a house or lot.

---

*From Historic Districts Zoning Regulations, Macon, Georgia.

Beacon Hill Architectural Handbook

Beacon Hill Civic Association

Notes on sign design. (Excerpted from the Boston Sign Code)

This sense of history and feeling of architectural unity is one of Boston's unique characteristics; it is attractive to both tourists and residents alike. And although nothing in the long run can replace the quality and character of a business concern's services or merchandise in drawing and keeping customers, the architecture of an individual building—and the combined impact of groups of adjoining buildings—can be part of the attraction of a shopping district.

Ideally, then, to maximize the effectiveness of signs and building architecture, every sign should be an integral—but, of course, noticeable—part of its building, and each building should be a good neighbor within its block of buildings. As a result, the building and its sign become part of an overall image, each supporting the other and helping to draw customers.

This leads to a simple but vital point: a sign on a building should always be thought of as part of the building and not as an unrelated object attached to it.

Design criteria established by the Architectural Commission are as follows:

1. Graphics shall be limited to a single sign, excluding the introduction of a projecting symbol.

2. Overhanging signs are generally discouraged except in the case where a flat sign cannot be appropriately mounted.

3. Trademarks shall be limited to 25 percent of sign area.

4. Paper signs attached to windows (announcing sales, etc.) are discouraged and under no circumstances are to be allowed beyond 15 days.

5. Lighting: back-lit signs are not allowed and shielded indirect lighting should be encouraged.

6. Location: should be integrated architecturally with the building, or on an awning in accordance with the zoning code limitations. In no case should a sign applied to the building obscure architectural detailing on the building face.

7. Restoration of free-standing signs is discouraged.

In closing, something should be said about two of the most important aspects of sign design—the choice of colors and the choice of lettering. A few basic rules may help to simplify the task of choosing from the almost unlimited range of colors and letter styles available:

1. Do not use too many colors on a sign. Too many colors can work against each other and detract from the strength of a sign's visual image. A simple combination of black and/or white and a single well-chosen color is often the most striking and effective.

2. Try to relate the general color effect of the sign to the building to which it belongs.

3. Choose a style of letter that is appropriate to the business and building (preferably no more than one style per sign).

4. Make sure that the letters are closely legible, whatever style is chosen, or they will not be doing their job. It should be emphasized that the greatest legibility is not necessarily the result of the largest size letters.

5. Choose the size of the letters carefully. Just as the sign should be in proportion to its building, the size of the letters should be in proportion—both to the sign and the building.

A note on existing signs. (Excerpted from the Boston Sign Code)

If there is an old, existing sign on the building that is still appropriate to the business, make sure that it is not of historic interest or aesthetic merit before replacing it. Many signs dating from around the turn of the century still exist and, when restored, can contribute character and distinction to the business, building, and the street.

Appendix F*

Demolition Criteria

1. Demolition

It is the policy of this Commission to encourage the preservation of historic structures, sites, and areas and to protect against the razing or demolition of any building or structure which is listed in the National Register of Historic Places or rated number 1 or number 2 in the Macon Historic Building Survey published by the Middle Georgia Historical Society, or which constitute a part of the historic fabric of the neighborhood.

  (a) The Historic Advisory Board on receipt of any application for a Certificate of Appropriateness to raze or demolish a building, structure, or any part thereof shall initially review the circumstances and the condition of the structure or part proposed for demolition and make an initial determination as to whether any of the following criteria apply to the structure:

    (i)   Is the building of such architectural or historical interest that its removal would be to the detriment of the public interest;

    (ii)   Is the building of such old and unusual or uncommon design, texture and material that it could not be reproduced or be reproduced only with great difficulty;

    (iii) Would retention of the building help preserve and protect an historic place or area of historic interest in the County; and/or

    (iv) Would retention of the building promote the general welfare by maintaining and increasing real estate values; generating business; creating new positions attracting tourists, students, writers, historians, artists and artisans; attracting new residents; encouraging study and interest in American history; stimulating interest and study in architecture and design; educating citizens in American culture and heritage; or making the County a more attractive and desirable place in which to live?

  (b) Should the Historic Advisory Board determine that none of the criteria listed above are present, it shall immediately recommend to the Commission that a Certificate of Appropriateness be issued. However, should the Historic Advisory Board determine that at least one of the criteria above exists, the procedures set out in Section 21.13[3] (c) and (d) below shall apply;

  (c) The Board shall notify persons or groups interested in historic

---

*From Historic Districts Zoning Regulations, Macon, Georgia.

preservation who may wish to work with the owner or applicant in an effort to preserve the structure, or locate purchasers who would agree to preserve the building or structure in accordance with the provisions of this section;

(d) The Board prior to the expiration of a one-hundred-eighty (180) day period must make a report to the Commission concerning its efforts to preserve the structure. If efforts at preservation fail, the Commission, following receipt of the report, shall issue a Certificate of Appropriateness;

(e) No Certificate of Appropriateness shall be issued for the razing or demolition of any structure listed in the National Register of Historic Places or rated number 1 or number 2 in the Macon Historic Building Survey published by the Middle Georgia Historical Society;

(f) The razing or demolition of any building or structure or any part thereof located in an historic district without first obtaining a Certificate of Appropriateness from the Commission shall subject such person to the penalties provided for in Chapter 33 of this Resolution. In addition, the Commission may refuse to grant a permit for new construction or for land use for a period of two (2) years, or condition the granting of any permit for new construction of land use as would best serve the purposes of this chapter.

2. Demolition Criteria

(a) Upon receipt of an application for Certificate of Appropriateness for demolition, the Planning Commission shall as soon as possible make a determination, supported by written findings, whether one or more of the following criteria are met:

(1) The structure is of such interest or quality that it would reasonably meet national, state, or local criteria for designation as an historic or architectural landmark.

(2) The structure is of such unusual or uncommon design texture or materials that it could not be reproduced or be reproduced only with great difficulty and expense.

(3) Retention of the structure would aid substantially in preserving and protecting a structure which meets criteria (1) and (2) hereinabove.

Where the Planning Commission determines that one or more of these criteria are met, no Certificate of Appropriateness shall be issued and the application shall be denied. (Los Angeles, California, Ordinance No. 152-422, Section 1 (F) (4) (b)).

3. The Board of Supervisors shall consider any or all of the following criteria in determining whether or not to grant a permit for razing or demolition.

(a) Is the building or structure of such architectural or historic interest that its removal would be to the detriment of the public interests?

(b) Is the building or structure of such interest or significance that it could be made into a national, state, or local historic shrine?

(c) Is the building of such old and unusual or uncommon design, texture and/or material that it could not be reproduced or be reproduced only with great difficulty and/or expense?

(d) Would retention of the building or structure help preserve and protect an historic place or area of historic interest in the county?

(e) Would retention of the building or structure promote the general welfare of the county by encouraging study of American history, architecture, and design or by developing an understanding of the importance and value of the American culture and heritage as well as by making the county a more attractive and desirable place in which to live? (Louden County, Virginia, Ordinance, Section 750.15.1.)

Appendix G

Minimum Maintenance Requirements

1. Protective maintenance of historic buildings. Historic buildings shall be maintained to meet the requirements of the Minimum Housing Code and the Building Code. (Savannah, Georgia, Ordinance, Section 9 (4).)
2. The board of architectural review, on its own initiative, may file a petition with the public safety and housing officer requesting that said officer proceed under the public safety and housing ordinance to require correction of defects or repairs to any structure covered by this article so that such structure shall be preserved and protected in consonance with the purpose of this article and the public safety and housing ordinance. (Charleston, South Carolina, Ordinance, Section 51-31.)
3. All buildings and structures in that section of the city known as the Vieux Carre Section and so defined generally in Section 65-6, Section 65-7, under the jurisdiction of the Vieux Carre Commission, as provided by Article 14 of Section 22A of the Louisiana Constitution, shall be preserved against decay and deterioration and kept free from certain structural defects in the following manner, by the owner thereof or such other person or persons who may have the legal custody and control thereof. The owner and other person having legal custody and control thereof shall repair such building if it is found to have any of the following defects:

    (a) Those which have parts thereof which are so attached that they may fall and injure members of the public or property.

    (b) Deteriorated or inadequate foundation.

    (c) Defective or deteriorated flooring or floor supports or flooring or floor supports of insufficient size to carry imposed loads with safety.

    (d) Members of walls, partitions, or other vertical supports that split, lean, list, or buckle due to defective material or deterioration.

    (e) Members of walls, partitions, or other vertical supports that are of insufficient size to carry imposed loads with safety.

    (f) Members of ceilings, roofs, ceiling and roof supports, or other horizontal members which sag, split or buckle due to defective material or deterioration.

    (g) Members of ceilings, roofs, ceiling and roof supports, or other horizontal members that are of insufficient size to carry imposed loads with safety.

    (h) Fireplaces or chimneys which list, bulge, or settle due to defective material or deterioration.

    (i) Fireplaces or chimneys which are of insufficient size or strength to carry imposed loads with safety.

(j) Deteriorated, crumbling, or loose plaster.

(k) Deteriorated or ineffective waterproofing of exterior walls, roofs, foundations, or floors, including broken windows or doors.

(l) Defective or lack of weather protection for exterior wall coverings, including lack of paint, or weathering due to lack of paint or other protective covering.

(m) Any fault or defect in the building which renders the same structurally unsafe or not properly weather tight. (New Orleans, Louisiana, Vieux Carre, Ordinance, Section 65-36.)

Appendix H

Question and Answer Brochure

For use in public relations campaign designed to inform citizens of the exact nature of a proposed historic preservation ordinance.

Q. What is an historic district?

A. This is a locally designated area in which any proposed plans for major exterior alterations, new construction, or demolition must be reviewed and receive a Certificate of Appropriateness. Proposed plans will be reviewed on the basis of (1) general compatibility with the surrounding neighborhood; (2) enhancement, rather than diminishment, of the architectural and historic value of the structure; (3) respect of the integrity of the architectural style of the structure.

Q. Do I have a choice about whether or not my property is included in an historic district?

A. An historic district will not be imposed upon a neighborhood against the wishes of a majority of the people who own property in the area. When an area is recommended for historic district designation, a public hearing will be held so that the views of property owners can be heard.

Q. What if an historic district is created and, at a later date, I decide I don't like it?

A. If a majority of the property owners petition the City Council for repeal, the ordinance can be appealed. In addition, the City Council has the right to appeal any ordinance at its own discretion.

Q. If my house is in an historic district, do I have to open it to public tours?

A. Absolutely not. There is no public access involved.

Q. If my property is in an historic district, can I still operate it as an apartment house?

A. Designation of historic districts has no effect upon zoning or land use. It is a zoning ordinance that determines how a property may be used.

Q. If my property is in an historic district, will I have to pay an extra tax?

A. Historic districts *are* somewhat like an improvement district, but without the taxing authority. There is no extra tax imposed upon an historic district. Instead, you may be able to qualify for certain federal tax benefits.

Q. Will I be required to make improvements to my house?

A. Being within an historic district does not require property owners to do any work on their house they were not planning to do anyway. No one can force you to make changes unless you want to make changes.

Q. What about the interior of my house?

A. The ordinance will have absolutely no control over the interior of any building.

Q. Will the Commission review minor repairs to my house?

A. No. Ordinary maintenance, or repair, of any exterior feature that does not involve a physical change of design and, thus, does not require a building permit, will not need a Certificate of Appropriateness.

Q. If I am building a new structure, does it have to be of historic design?

A. No. There will be nothing in the guidelines to preclude contemporary architecture. The Historic Preservation Commission will review the plans for any proposed construction to ensure that it will be *compatible* with the surrounding neighborhood and not have a negative influence.

Q. What if I am denied a Certificate of Appropriateness?

A. You may, within fifteen days after the making of such a decision, appeal to the Mayor and Council and, if not satisfied with their action, then appeal to the Superior Court.

Q. What if I do not receive a Certificate of Appropriateness and do what I want to do anyway?

A. You will be guilty of a misdemeanor.

Q. Will the controls in an historic district make it more difficult to sell my property?

A. Not at all. The neighborhood will be enhanced and, thereby, so will your property. Experience with other historic districts has shown a strong improvement in the housing market within historic district areas. There are no limitations set on the sale of property by the Historic Preservation Ordinance.

Q. What does the establishment of an historic district do to my property values?

A. We don't know for every individual case. However, the evidence from other historic districts indicates that property values are generally found to stabilize or increase.

Q. Historic districts seem like a lot of trouble. Is it worth it?

A. There will actually be very little inconvenience caused to the average property owner and, as a result, the entire historic district will be maintained and improved as a desirable place to live and as a unique area of special interest. The Historic Preservation Ordinance will help us maintain the special contribution which this area's historic architecture makes to our community. A richness and a diversity are added to our lives by the presence of an historic district through the maintenance of a living example of some of the finer elements of our American heritage.

Why Do We Want An Historic District?

1. It will have a strong stabilizing effect on the investment the property owner has in his property. Neighborhoods go through a cycle. When a neighborhood is new, there is a growth stage. The demand is high, the supply low, and hence property values are also high. At some point an equilibrium stage is reached and, due to age and other factors, property values tend to fall off. Unless some outside influence is injected on the downward slide, property values will continue to fall. By and large, historic districts established across the country have been the outside influence that has stopped neighborhoods from continuing on their downward slide. Values tend to bottom out and begin to increase again.
2. The assurance that the distinctiveness of the area will be protected will encourage many property owners and residents of the neighborhood to improve their property and spur many on to seek further improvements such as cleaner streets, better lighting, and other increases in public services.
3. It will be a factor in encouraging the restoration of structures of historic or architectural importance within the districts and guard against their demolition, thus making it unnecessary to turn such buildings into tax exempt museums in order to assure their preservation.
4. Protection of the character and continuity of the district will be assured by introducing a design review of new construction in the area, making sure the integrity remains intact. Is the roof design compatible with the buildings? Is the building tall and thin while the surrounding area is all horizontal? How do the height, scale, spaces, etc., relate to what is going on in the immediate vicinity?
5. It will insure the architectural integrity of the proposed historic district by reviewing any proposed plans for major exterior alterations or demolition so as to avoid further changes that will have an adverse effect on that area.
6. The proposed historic district is close to downtown. For this reason there have been many incompatible intrusions into the area. It is obvious that existing zoning could benefit from the support of a case by case—much closer—design review process included in a historic district ordinance. The neighborhood will be better able to protect and preserve the architectural and historic integrity of the area and stop unwanted changes and intrusions. If the neighborhood does not band together, bit by bit, there will be an erosion of one sort or another. It is a judgment each property owner will have to make as to whether he or

she likes some of the changes that are happening generally, or whether everyone together can work more creatively.

Appendix I

Sources of Assistance

National Trust for Historic Preservation
1785 Massachusetts Avenue, N.W.
Washington, D.C. 20036
(202) 673-4000
—for information about legal questions and review procedures.

The Southern Regional Office of the Trust responds to requests for information and advice, including on-site consultations in the southern states of Georgia, Florida, South Carolina, North Carolina, Tennessee, Kentucky, Alabama, Mississippi, Louisiana, and Arkansas. The southern regional office address is:

> 456 King Street
> Charleston, South Carolina 29403
> (803) 724-4711

National Alliance of Preservation Commissions
Suite 500, 1522 K Street, N.W.
Washington, D.C. 20052

—for information regarding operational standards, how others have handled problem areas, training programs, and other commissions in your area.

State Historic Preservation Office
Historic Preservation Section
Georgia Department of Natural Resources
270 Washington Street, S.W.
Room 701
Atlanta, Georgia 30334
(404) 656-2840; GIST 221-2840

The Historic Preservation Section administers the National Register program in Georgia and works with the National Park Service in implementing the National Historic Preservation Act of 1966 and the Economic Recovery Tax Act of 1981.

The Historic Preservation Section provides information and technical assistance on National Register nominations, certified rehabilitation projects, and performs an environmental review function. It also provides preservation planning assistance both directly and through a Regional Preservation Planner Program in coordination with area planning commissions. On the next pages is a list of area commissions and the counties they serve.

GEORGIA APDCs

ALTAMAHA GEORGIA SOUTHERN
APDC
P.O. Box 328
Baxley, GA 31513
(912) 367-3648; GIST 366-5260

Counties:

Appling	Jeff Davis
Bulloch	Tattnall
Candler	Toombs
Evans	Wayne

*ATLANTA REGIONAL COMMISSION
230 Peachtree St., N.W.
Suite 200
Atlanta, GA 30303
(404) 656-7700; GIST 221-7700

Counties:

Cobb	Fulton
Clayton	Gwinnett
DeKalb	Rockdale
Douglas	

*CENTRAL SAVANNAH RIVER APDC
P.O. Box 2800
Augusta, GA 30904
(404) 828-2356; GIST 331-2356

Counties:

Burke	McDuffie
Columbia	Richmond
Emanuel	Screven
Glascock	Taliaferro
Jefferson	Warren
Jenkins	Wilkes
Lincoln	

CHATTAHOOCHEE-FLINT APDC
P.O. Box 2308
Newnan, GA 30264
(404) 253-8521

Counties:

Carroll	Meriwether
Coweta	Troup
Heard	

COASTAL APDC
P.O. Drawer 1917
Brunswick, GA 31521
(912) 264-7363; GIST 365-7363

Counties:

Bryan	Glynn
Camden	Liberty
Chatham	Long
Effingham	McIntosh

*COOSA VALLEY APDC
P.O. Drawer H
Rome, GA 30161
(404) 295-6485; GIST 231-6485

Counties:

Bartow	Gordon
Catoosa	Haralson
Chattooga	Paulding
Dade	Polk
Floyd	Walker

GEORGIA MOUNTAINS APDC
P.O. Box 1720
Gainesville, GA 30501
(404) 536-3431 or 532-7261

Counties:

Banks	Lumpkin
Dawson	Rabun
Forsyth	Stephens
Habersham	Union
Hall	White
Hart	

*HEART OF GEORGIA APDC
501 Oak Street
Eastman, GA 31023
(912) 374-4771; GIST 327-6403

Counties:

Bleckley	Telfair
Dodge	Treutlen
Laurens	Wheeler
Montgomery	Wilcox
Pulaski	

LOWER CHATTAHOOCHEE APDC
P.O. Box 1908
Columbus, GA 31902
(404) 259-7468

Counties:

Chattahoochee	Quitman
Clay	Randolph
Harris	Stewart
Muscogee	Talbot

*MCINTOSH TRAIL APDC
P.O. Box 241
Griffin, GA 30224
(404) 227-3096

Counties:

Butts	Newton
Fayette	Pike
Henry	Spalding
Lamar	Upson

MIDDLE FLINT APDC
P.O. Box 6
Ellaville, GA 31806
(912) 937-2561; GIST 345-1204

Counties:

Crisp	Schley
Dooly	Sumter
Macon	Taylor
Marion	Webster

*MIDDLE GEORGIA APDC
711 Grand Building
Macon, GA 31201
(912) 744-6160; GIST 321-6160

Counties:

Bibb	Monroe
Crawford	Peach
Houston	Twiggs
Jones	

*NORTH GEORGIA APDC
503 West Waugh Street
Dalton, GA 30720
(404) 272-2300; GIST 234-2300

Counties:

Cherokee	Murray
Fannin	Pickens
Gilmer	Whitfield

NORTHEAST GEORGIA APDC
305 Research Drive
Athens, GA 30605
(404) 548-3141

Counties:

Barrow	Madison
Clarke	Morgan
Elbert	Oconee
Greene	Oglethorpe
Jackson	Walton

*OCONEE APDC
P.O. Box 707
Milledgeville, GA 31061
(912) 453-5327; GIST 324-5327

Counties:

Baldwin	Putnam
Hancock	Washington
Jasper	Wilkinson
Johnson	

SOUTH GEORGIA APDC
P.O. Box 1223
Valdosta, GA 31601
(912) 247-3494; GIST 343-3494

Counties:

Ben Hill	Irwin
Berrien	Lanier
Brooks	Lowndes
Cook	Tift
Echols	Turner

*SOUTHEAST GEORGIA APDC
P.O. Box 2049
Waycross, GA 31501
(912) 285-6097; GIST 368-6097

Counties:

Atkinson	Clinch
Bacon	Coffee
Brantley	Pierce
Charlton	Ware

*SOUTHWEST GEORGIA APDC
P.O. Box 346
Camilla, GA 31730
(912) 336-5616; GIST 341-4315

Counties:

Baker	Lee
Calhoun	Miller
Colquitt	Mitchell
Decatur	Seminole
Dougherty	Terrell
Early	Thomas
Grady	Worth

The regions marked with an asterisk (*) do not have a preservation planner. Please contact the Historic Preservation Section for assistance in those regions.

Georgia Trust for Historic Preservation
1516 Peachtree Street, N.W.
Atlanta, Georgia 30309
(404) 881-9980

—provides information and educational programs.

The University of Georgia

Institute of Community and Area Development
300 Old College
The University of Georgia
Athens, Georgia 30602
(404) 542-3350; GIST 241-3350

—provides information, technical assistance, and educational programs.

Historic Preservation Program
School of Environmental Design
The University of Georgia
Athens, Georgia 30602
(404) 542-1816; GIST 241-1816

—provides information and technical assistance.

INDEX

280001

DATE DUE

The Library Store #47-0152